Creating an Investment Policy Statement

Creating an Investment Policy Statement

Guidelines & Templates

Norman M. Boone, MBA, CFP®

Linda S. Lubitz, CFP®

The Financial Planning Association (FPA) is the membership association for the financial planning community. FPA is committed to providing information and resources to help financial planners and those who champion the financial planning process succeed. And, FPA believes that everyone needs objective advice to make smart financial decisions.

FPA Press is the publishing arm of FPA, providing current content and advanced thinking on technical and practice management topics.

Information in this book is accurate as of the time of publication and consistent with standards of good practice in the financial planning community. As research and practice advance, however, standards may change. For this reason, it is recommended that readers evaluate the applicability of any recommendation in light of particular situations and changing standards.

Financial Planning Association
4100 Mississippi Ave., Suite 400
Denver Colorado 80246-3053

Phone: 800.322.4237
fax: 303.759.0749
email: fpapress@fpanet.org

www.fpanet.org

ISBN: 0-9753448-0-3

Manufactured in the United States of America

Published in association with AdvisorPress
www.advisorpress.com
408.400.0400

*This book is dedicated to all those who have supported,
inspired, and laughed with us over the years—far too many to
individually name. We have been blessed.
Special thanks to our respective staff teams:
Dave, Kevin, Rahel, Sabrina, Holly, Mary, Jennifer, Alda, and Juliet;
Ami, Maria, Freddy, and Penny.*

*Our Capstone Study Group has provided
encouragement, friendship, and inspirations.*

*And lastly, a toast to collaboration—
it has brought joy and new dimensions to our lives.*

*OK, OK, just had to give a few more specific names:
Marv Tuttle, for publishing our first joint article on this topic.
Carl Gargula, for being the thoughtful founding father
for the idea to write a book.
Bob Veres, for his continuing support.*

Thank you all.

About the Authors

Norman M. Boone, MBA, CFP®, is the
president of Boone Financial Advisors,
Inc., a San Francisco-based financial planning and investment management firm. He
began his career in the financial services
industry as a banker, served as a CFO for
two regional operating companies and
began his financial planning practice in
1987. He has served on the national board
of directors of the Financial Planning
Association, on the advisory council for Schwab Institutional and for
the TIAA-CREF Institute. Norm has written articles for and given
talks to consumers and the financial services industry on investment,
practice management, fiduciary practices and financial planning
topics. He is a former columnist for the *Journal of Financial Planning*
and for the *Journal of Retirement Planning*. He has been cited as
one of the top financial advisors in the country by *Worth* magazine,
Medical Economics, Mutual Funds magazine and *Bloomberg Wealth
Manager*.

Norm lives in Oakland, California, with his partner, Linda Lubitz.
He has two college-age children and enjoys the time he can spend
with them, as well as participating in his community and traveling to
places around the world. He can be reached at
NBoone@BooneAdvisors.com.

Linda S. Lubitz, CFP®, is the President of The Lubitz Financial Group in Miami, Florida, and also the managing director of Boone Financial Advisors, East Bay Region. She has had over 30 years' experience in the financial services industry with such firms as AmeriFirst Bank, AmeriFirst Securities Corporation (which she founded and was president), and Evensky & Brown Financial Advisors.

Her professional accomplishments have included being elected to the national board of directors for the International Association for Financial Planning and subsequently to the Financial Planning Association board. She is an emeritus member of the TIAA-CREF Institute Advisory Board and Florida Bankers Trust School faculty. Many financial publications, such as *Worth* magazine, *Medical Economics, Bloomberg Wealth Manager* and *Mutual Funds* magazine have named Linda as one of the top advisors on their annual lists, and she continues to receive recognition both locally and nationally for her contribution to the community and to the profession.

Linda lives in Miami, Florida, with her four cats and in Oakland, California, with her partner, Norm Boone. She feels truly blessed to have found a life work in which she can make a difference in people's lives, use her teaching and quantitative skills while running a profitable business. She hopes that readers of this book will find their highest and best use in life and live their dreams.

Linda and Norm successfully summitted Mount Kilimanjaro, Tanzania in January, 2004.

She can be reached at LindaL@LubitzFinancial.com.

Preface

THE INVESTMENT POLICY STATEMENT (IPS) should be the basic building block in an intentional investment process. In creating an IPS, the investment manager and the client agree upon all of the essential issues surrounding how and why the money is to be managed in a particular way. The IPS development process provides a crucial education process for the client and is a key communication step, helping each party to understand the other's perspective and goals. The IPS is the document that guides the investment manager in making future decisions, while serving as a guidepost against which the reality of what has happened can be measured against the rules, procedures and benchmarks that were previously agreed to. Finally, it serves to create a purposeful decision-making process in rational times in order to guide clients through the inevitable rough periods when emotions cause us all to make less than optimal decisions.

We believe that investment advisors should create and maintain an Investment Policy Statement for each and every client they work with. Being intentional about the advice you give and documenting it can only help you succeed as a professional.

It is our hope that the first half of this book will help you appreciate the process in developing an Investment Policy Statement as well as the issues that should be addressed by you and your client and then documented. The second half of the book provides examples of different Investment Policy Statements for eight different kinds of clients. Some of the wording is shared from one type to another. Some is unique to each respective client. We've tried to show these differences, as well as some of the differences that might be exhibited between different advisors with different approaches. We've also provided you with a sample questionnaire and some resources to which you can refer.

We hope you will use this material to make your practice better and more successful.

Norm Boone and Linda Lubitz

x

Table of Contents

Introduction

IN 1996, CARL GARGULA, then president of Ibbotson Associates, came to us with an idea. Over the prior years, we had written a few articles and given a few speeches on the importance of using an Investment Policy Statement in our investment process. Carl suggested that we bring our material to Ibbotson, a well-respected investment consulting, research and publishing firm, so that together we could create a software product to help advisors create their own Investment Policy Statements. We enthusiastically agreed.

Unfortunately, Carl soon afterward left Ibbotson. "The Investment Policy Statement Guidebook" was developed first as a series of templates and later using a standard document individualized through a series of Microsoft "wizards." This was a good solution, but not the ultimate one.

With that history in mind, and based on our vision and desire to help our colleagues, we decided to create a better aid to those wanting to develop Investment Policy Statements for their clients. Hence, *Creating an Investment Policy Statement.* We hope it serves you well. If you have ideas or suggestions, we'd very much like to hear from you:

Norman M. Boone
Boone Financial Advisors Inc.
415-788-1952
nboone@BooneAdvisors.com

Linda Lubitz
The Lubitz Financial Group
305-670-4440
LindaL@LubitzFinancial.com

Please check out our IPS development tool at **www.ipsadvisorpro.com**.

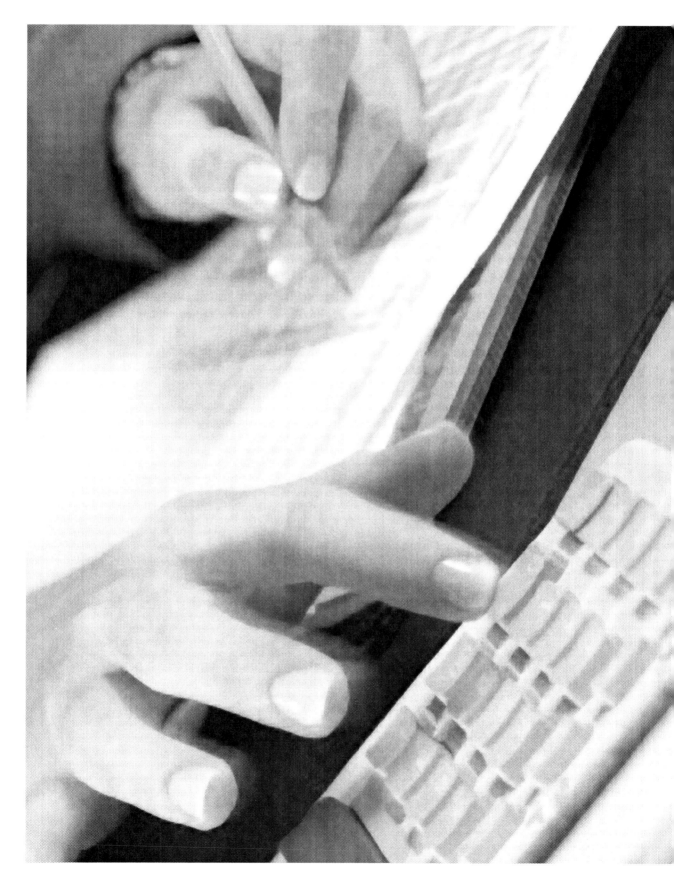

What Is an Investment Policy Statement?

Overview

THERE HAS BEEN A REVOLUTION recently in the world of investing. Though it has been a quiet revolution, it has created a profound influence on how investment decisions are being made. At the center of this revolution is a major national trend in the law affecting situations in which fiduciary responsibilities are involved. These legal changes have arisen in response to changing economic conditions, newer investment vehicles and strategies, modern investment theory, and an evolving regulatory environment for fiduciaries ("fiduciaries" are generally people charged with making investment decisions for the benefit of others).

The Investment Policy Statement should be the basic building block in an intentional investment process.

With the enactment of the Employee Retirement Income and Security Act (ERISA) of 1974, plan fiduciaries became liable for breaches in prudent investing and diversification standards. (ERISA represents the rules and regulations under which most private-sector employee benefit plans operate. Many of the plans involve assets set aside for the employee's future use. Such ERISA employee benefit plans include 401(k) plans, profit-sharing and other defined-contribution plans, pension and other defined-benefit plans and VEBAs.)

Internal Revenue Code Section 402(b)(1), also known as ERISA, states, "Every employee benefit plan shall provide a procedure for establishing and carrying out a funding policy and method consistent with the objectives of the plan and requirement of this title." Thus was born the requirement for Investment Policy Statements. Virtually all sophisticated investors now use Investment Policy Statements.

The Investment Policy Statement should be the basic building block in an intentional investment process. The client has a right to know what the investment manager is going to do and how decisions are to be made. If the client has particular directives, the investment manager had better know about them ahead of time. By writing down this information, both parties clarify their expectations and decrease the likelihood of frustration with the other. There are clearly some benefits to this process:

1. The process of establishing the investment policies to be followed offers the best possible opportunity to educate the client about the investment issues to be faced and why the advisor follows the selected approach.

2. The process provides a ready-made forum for the all-important communication between client and advisor.

3. The IPS provides a guide to the advisor for making all future investment decisions for the client.

4. The IPS provides to the client a means of measuring the advisor—has the advisor done as promised?

5. The IPS represents a set of policies, created in a rational setting, which can serve as a moderating influence on the client who tends to want to jump from one idea to the next, or to emotionally react when markets are volatile.

An Investment Policy Statement is a document crafted for a specific investor (an individual, employee benefit plan, endowment, foundation or trust). It is a statement of the investor's investment philosophy and investment goals while also establishing the investment management procedures. The Investment Policy Statement provides the foundation for all future investment decisions the investor makes. It serves as a guidepost for the investment decision makers, creating a system and a discipline for all future investment decisions.

Because the IPS is intended to provide a guideline for future decision making, it needs to be a written document rather than simply a verbal agreement. At the same time, it is not intended to be a contract. Rather, it should be seen as a directive from the client to the investment manager stating how the client's assets are to be managed. Because the investment manager is likely to have a greater familiarity with the content and format of an IPS, the investment advisor most often prepares it with input from the client. To signal its importance, the client should sign it.

It is imperative for the advisor to remember that (1) it is essential to have a written policy statement and (2) it is vital if you have one to *follow it!* The worst possible consequence exists if you have one and don't follow it.

The IPS is a statement of the investor's investment philosophy and investment goals while also establishing the investment management procedures.

The Role of the IPS

The Investment Policy Statement serves four basic purposes:

1. **Setting Objectives** — To establish clear and definable expectations, risk and return objectives, and guidelines for the investment of the assets.

2. **Defining the Asset Allocation Policy** — To set forth a structure and identify the investment asset classes to use to achieve

The IPS should be able to provide an important record of why and how things were done.

a diversified portfolio, as well as to determine how those assets are to be best allocated toward the achievement of the investor's objectives.

3. **Establishing Management Procedures** — To provide a guide for selecting, monitoring, and evaluating the performance of those charged with managing and investing the assets, as well as making changes as appropriate.

4. **Determining Communication Procedures** — To provide a concise method of communicating the process and objectives among all parties involved with the investments, while assigning responsibility for implementation.

For the typical investor, a lack of information, the absence of a systematic approach, and emotional and behavioral factors often lead to irrational or inappropriate investment decisions. The creation and use of an IPS helps clients and advisors make prudent, rational decisions about their investments. This process will generally help both the investor and the advisor become better and more successful in their respective roles.

The IPS should provide a record of the investor's mindset— objectives, concerns, circumstances and expectations. Having such a record can provide important legal protection for those fiduciaries and decision makers who might become subject to lawsuits and other conflicts. The IPS should be able to provide an important record of why and how things were done. While the results may or may not have been desirable, if the process was a reasonable one, courts have shown an unwillingness to side with plaintiffs so long as a prudent system and discipline were followed for investment decisions.

The Benefits of Using an Investment Policy Statement

Using a properly composed Investment Policy Statement should bring the following benefits:

- An IPS compels the investor and the investor's advisor to be more disciplined and systematic in their decision making, which in itself should improve the odds of meeting the investment goals.

- Objectives and expectations are clear for all concerned parties.

- Misunderstandings are more likely to be avoided.

- Approved procedures are specified so everyone concerned will know what to expect.

- Decisions can be made as to how things will be done under a variety of circumstances in a deliberate fashion, rather than in the "heat of battle." Planning ahead makes it easier for all when the environment gets stormy.

- The Investment Policy Statement establishes a record of decisions and an objective means to test whether those serving the investor are complying with the investor's requirements.

- The IPS provides a ready means to communicate to advisors, beneficiaries, and current and future fiduciaries how the investor proposes to go about acting upon his/her/their duties.

Who Needs an Investment Policy Statement?

Every investor needs an investment policy. In certain instances, having it in writing is mandatory by law. (We think it should always be in writing.)

When is it mandated by law? In general, an investment policy is required anytime a person or group is making investment decisions for the benefit of others, regardlesss of whether the decision makers also have a direct personal interest in the assets. For example:

- When the investments are subject to ERISA

- When the investments are subject to a Taft-Hartley plan

- When the investments are held in some kind of trust for the benefit, now or in the future, of any person or any entity other than the trustees

- When the investments are owned by a foundation or endowment

- When the funds are in an estate and the executor(s) is making investment decisions

- When investment decisions need to be made and there are one or more persons acting in a fiduciary capacity, especially in those states that have passed the Uniform Prudent Investor Act.

The one obvious exception is individual investors making decisions for themselves or their family. Even though it may not be legally mandated, we believe that all investors will benefit from designing and using an Investment Policy Statement.

We believe it is better to have an Investment Policy Statement than to not have one, for all the reasons discussed above. That being said, once you write down the policies, you have an obligation to follow them. Be very careful about what is written, because if you do not adhere to the policies you set out for your client, you would have been better off not having written them at all!

And lastly, should you be affiliated with a broker-dealer, you may want to talk with your compliance department about what they will require with regard to Investment Policy Statements.

Do you Need an Investment Policy Statement? — A Quiz for the Investor

Try answering these questions:

1. What is your target rate of return? Is it a nominal rate or in relation to some benchmark, such as inflation or the S&P 500?

2. What rate of return have your investments achieved over the last three years? Last five years?

3. How are the returns calculated?

4. Are you a "fiduciary"?

5. What procedures do you use to select your investments or your investment managers (or funds)?

6. What is your investment allocation?

7. What system, if any, do you use to rebalance your portfolio?

8. Which asset classes are permitted for your use? Which are restricted?

9. What level of risk is acceptable to you and how do you quantify that?

10. How much liquidity is required for your portfolio and how do you determine that level?

If your client's response to any of the above was "I don't know,"
if their answer was less than clear, or if they answered "yes" to
question 4, then your client needs an Investment Policy Statement
and this book is intended for you.

Why Bother?

The Successful Advisory Relationship

What is it that makes one client relationship work and another one not? We think four critical pieces determine the success of each relationship:

1. **The client gets what is expected.**

   Clients always have some idea of what it is that they want from an advisor. While that set of desires may change over time, if clients are not getting what they want and expect from an advisor, they are not going to be pleased about the relationship. Striving to create "Raving Fans"* out of your clients means that you need to meet their needs and their reasonable expectations (and probably give them more). You can help shape their expectations and help align them with their needs, but if you are not going to satisfy their expectations, the relationship will probably not last long enough to allow that to happen.

2. **The client understands and is pleased with the various aspects of the engagement.**

   If clients don't at least understand the basics of what you are providing them, it's only luck if they are pleased with what they are getting. If you help them to understand what you need to do to help them meet their goals and how you are going to work to help them achieve those goals, then they are likely to be pleased. If clients really understand what you are doing, why you are doing it and that you are making recommendations in their best interests, almost certainly they will be pleased with the relationship.

3) **The client accepts and implements the advice.**

   You can provide the best advice in the world, but if it doesn't get used, the opportunity is wasted. Clients who resist taking

---

* *Raving Fans,* Ken Blanchard and Sheldon Books, William Morrow & Co., 1992.

advice, or even those who do so reluctantly, are signaling that either you are giving them something other than what they expected or that they don't understand your recommendations. Successful relationships involve good advice and the implementation of that advice. Any other way and it won't work.

4) **The relationship is profitable and beneficial for both.**
   As an advisor, you need to earn an income so you can keep offering advice to your clients. The product of your advice should result in your clients being in a better place than they would have been without your advice. In addition, it greatly helps if both you and the client enjoy working together, identifying problems, seeking solutions and implementing them. The benefit to the clients is that their lives are improved— maybe they sleep better at night, maybe they are richer, maybe you have helped them do things they'd always wanted to do but hadn't thought they could afford to. The benefit to you is not only the revenue, but also that you enjoy what you are doing and that the feedback from clients (often in the form of referrals) is a positive reinforcement that you are making a meaningful difference in their lives.

Whether or not it is legally required, being thoughtful and systematic about how you do things will serve you well.

How Does a Successful Advisory Relationship Happen?

Providing advice that is meaningful, appropriate and beneficial to the client relies on several factors, but for the purposes of this discussion, we'd like to focus on two:

1. **You must clearly understand your client's goals.**
   We think this may be the most important part of any advisory relationship. Too often it is given perfunctory treatment or assumptions are made about what is wanted. In either case, what inevitably follow are inappropriate solutions and certain frustration from both your and your client's perspectives. We

Unless you probe, probe further and then probe again, you probably won't really understand what the client wants and needs.

will address this issue in greater detail later, but suffice it to say that unless you probe, probe further and then probe again, you probably won't really understand what the client wants and needs. Often the client may not have thought about your question or can't articulate their goals. (Note: while most of our comments are directed at individual clients or families, the rules apply to institutional clients as well.) You have to see their investment goals in the context of their current life and what they would like their life to be. Planning otherwise may keep them happy for a while, but eventually the relationship will sour because you haven't really understood or accomplished what was important to them. Spending more time up front and keeping up to date with your client afterward is the only solution.

2. **Clients want consistency from you, which strongly suggests the use of a systematic process for how you do things and how you make decisions.**

   One of the characteristics that inspires clients to have confidence in their advisor is the knowledge that the advisor would come to a similar decision/recommendation each time the question arose in similar circumstances. If you make it up as you go, clients won't know what to expect from you. They will begin to second-guess you because it would be clear in their minds that you don't have a well-developed approach to such a problem and aren't bringing any particular expertise to bear on the problem.

   In the case of investments, the process of how your recommendations are determined is telling. Are you simply recommending what's on the "hot" list now, or are there some underlying values and principles that guide you? If the latter, would you make similar recommendations to two clients who came to you at different times with similar circumstances and needs? To best serve your clients and to protect yourself from lawsuits, we believe it absolutely critical that your solutions for both follow a similar methodology, derived from the systems and processes guiding you.

With that in mind, we suggest the use of a "prudent investment process." Whether or not it is legally required, being thoughtful and systematic about how you do things will serve you well. Your clients will be better off for it, and as they recognize the benefits, the referrals they make and the additional money they bring to you will serve you well.

The History of Prudent Investing

As trusted advisors, we are fiduciaries.
We therefore must act like fiduciaries.

Are You a Fiduciary?

THE AMERICAN HERITAGE DICTIONARY defines a fiduciary as "a person who stands in a special relation of trust, confidence, or responsibility in his obligations to others…" Other definitions also find a fiduciary to be someone who:

- Holds discretionary authority or responsibility in plan or trust administration

- Exercises discretionary authority/control regarding management/disposition of plan assets

- Renders investment advice for a fee or other compensation

A fiduciary must follow a "prudent process."

In practical terms, a professional who is held in a capacity of trust who renders investment advice, or who has or exercises any discretionary authority or consistent influence over the client or the client's assets, is a fiduciary.

In our view, most financial advisors (except perhaps for the rare broker who calls his client only occasionally and has ideas often rejected) are fiduciaries.

So what are the implications of being a fiduciary?

- All decisions or recommendations made by a fiduciary on behalf of the client must be made solely in the interest of the client, which suggests you had better know what the client's interests are.

- A fiduciary must follow a "prudent process."

Since we must follow a prudent process, we had better know what a prudent process is.

The Evolution of the Prudent Investment Process

Harvard College v. Amory (1830)

The legal case that began the thoughtful evolution to what we know today as the prudent investment process was the *Harvard v. Amory* case of 1830. The issue at hand was: Can trustees invest assets in stocks? British law had established that the only permissible investment was government securities. The U.S. court found that since each trust has different needs and circumstances, the trustee must be relied upon to make appropriate decisions. They then set out to define what would be appropriate.

The *Harvard* case created the concept of the Prudent Man Rule. The court found that trustees should "observe how men of prudence, discretion and intelligence manage their own affairs, not in regard to speculation, but in regard to the permanent disposition of their funds, considering the probable income, as well as the probable safety of the capital to be invested."

This statement suggested certain criteria for how a trustee should behave. The trustee should:

- Exercise care in the selection of investments

- Exercise skill in making the selection

- Exercise the same caution that a reasonable person would exercise with his own investments

Not long after the *Harvard* case, the courts began to restrict its intended flexibility. "Legal lists" of permissible investments were soon created in most states. Trustees who ignored them, in effect, became personal guarantors against losses. In the development of these lists, stocks were generally presumed to be inappropriate investments and quality bonds were often the only assets that were permissible for investment of trust assets under trust law. For the most part, these were limited to government bonds as in British law. After the American Civil War, with the government in need of funds, this was an especially timely issue.

Depression Leads to New Approaches

In 1935, the American Law Institute (an arm of the American Bar Association) issued its first "Restatement of Trust Law" in which it attempted to consolidate all of the best thinking about trusts and the oversight of their assets as a guide for future law making and court decisions. This Restatement specifically permitted investment in conservative common stocks (in part because the market was rising by that time and trust beneficiaries stuck in bonds were missing out).

"Men of prudence, discretion and intelligence manage their own affairs, not in regard to speculation, but in regard to the permanent disposition of their funds, considering the probable income, as well as the probable safety of the capital to be invested."

The test of prudence should be the trustee's conduct, not the actual investment results.

In 1942, the American Bankers Association adopted the Model Prudent Man Investment Act. The act codified the flexibility intended in the *Harvard College* decision and permitted investment in stocks, bonds, real estate and mutual funds. By 1960 it had been adopted by most states.

Investment Theory and Understanding Evolved in the Post-WWII Era

In 1959, the Restatement (Second) of the Law of Trusts was issued. This Restatement reiterated support for the Prudent Man Rule, suggesting that as a trustee you should make investments as you would for yourself—concerned with both preservation of principal and income.

The Second Restatement also was notable in its position that the test of prudence should be the trustee's conduct, not the actual investment results. Nevertheless, the Restatement continued to prohibit use of "speculative investments" and the focus remained on individual investments.

Modern Portfolio Theory

Modern portfolio theory (MPT) concepts, developed during the 1950s and advanced over the years since then, won William Sharpe and Harry Markowitz a Nobel prize in 1990 for moving investment management from art to science. MPT addressed the construction of an optimal portfolio, suggesting that:

- Risk and return are related
- More diversification is important and desirable
- Markets are efficient
- Investors are generally risk averse

One of the critical principles on which Modern Portfolio Theory relied was that the whole portfolio must be considered when evaluating risk, so that if any particular investment should improve the risk/reward profile of the overall portfolio, it should be considered an appropriate investment, regardless of how risky it might seem on its own. As a result, the entire universe of investment vehicles should be considered available when building an optimal portfolio.

ERISA Moved Us into the 'Modern Era'

In 1974, the Employee Retirement Income and Security Act (ERISA), which was based on the principles of trust law but directed at corporate qualified retirement plans, made some critical breakthroughs in the acceptance of the newest theories about prudent investing.

ERISA recognized modern portfolio theory as the proper basis for judging the prudence of investment decisions. No longer were certain parts of the investment universe treated as beyond consideration and no investment was viewed as too risky, so long as its inclusion improved the total portfolio's risk and return profile.

ERISA required that an investment policy be in place. (Although there was no mention of it needing to be in writing, it is logical to assume that the only way to show that such a thing has been established and is in place is to be able to produce a written document describing the policies. The Department of Labor, which oversees qualified retirement plans, routinely has its agents ask for the written investment policy statement early in each plan audit it performs.)

ERISA also strengthened and reinforced the principle that conduct of the fiduciary and not investment performance should determine whether a fiduciary was to be considered prudent. Such conduct could be determined based on whether a reasonable investment policy was in place and being followed, if investment performance was being adequately monitored, if investment

No longer were certain parts of the investment universe considered beyond consideration and no investment was considered too risky, so long as its inclusion improved the total portfolio's risk and return profile.

In essence, ERISA virtually required that outside investment expertise be obtained.

expenses were being tightly controlled, if prohibited transactions were being avoided and if the liquidity necessary for planned as well as unexpected withdrawals was available.

The final contribution of ERISA was to raise the prudence standard from the Prudent Man Rule to "The Prudent Expert Rule." A "fiduciary shall discharge his duties with respect to a plan solely in the interest of the participants and beneficiaries and… with the care, skill, prudence, and diligence under the circumstances then prevailing that a prudent man acting in a like capacity and familiar with such matters would use in the conduct of an enterprise of like character and with like aims."

Ever since, it has no longer been sufficient to be careful. Since ERISA, you also had to be skilled at a level set by others in a similar capacity. In effect, ERISA was not only permitting but strongly encouraging plan trustees to delegate their duties of investment management functions to experts. This standard supplanted the "prudent layman" as to the definition of prudence. Under it the lack of relevant experience was not to be considered an excuse since appropriate expertise could have (and should have) been retained. In essence, ERISA virtually required that outside investment expertise be obtained.

The Uniform Prudent Investor Act

In 1992, the Restatement (Third) of Trust Law was issued. This Restatement was a comprehensive document that updated all the previous work on trusts and trust asset management, pulling in all of the newest ideas and principles.

In 1994, the Uniform Laws Commission approved the Third Restatement virtually verbatim. In effect, the wording of the Third Restatement became the Uniform Prudent Investor Act (UPIA), which has now been adopted by most states.

The key concepts promulgated by the Third Restatement and later by the UPIA were:

- The standard of prudence is applied to any investment as part of the total portfolio rather than to individual investments.

- The trade-off in all investing between risk and return is the fiduciary's central consideration.

- The trustee can invest in any investment that plays an appropriate role in achieving the risk/return objectives of the trust and that meets the other requirements of prudent investing.

- Diversification of investments is essential.

- Delegation of investment and management functions is now appropriate, subject to safeguards.

- Impartiality between current and future beneficiaries is required.

- Expenses must be controlled.

- Trustees are responsible for ascertaining all relevant facts.

The requirement that the trustees must consider all relevant factors was given greater detail, such that the following must specifically be part of the decision-making process:

- The possible effects of inflation/deflation

- The expected tax consequences

- The needs of *all* beneficiaries, both current and future

- The income and growth needs of current and future beneficiaries must be fairly balanced.

- The size of the portfolio

- The nature and duration of the fiduciary relationship

- Any liquidity and distribution requirements

- General economic conditions

- The expected total return of the portfolio

- The role each investment plays within the portfolio

An overall investment strategy must align with the risk tolerance and return objectives established by trustees. Because some level of risk is unavoidable, an appropriate risk/return trade-off reasonably suited to the circumstances must be established.

The principles and rules of the UPIA are considered the default state law. That is, where there is an explicit conflict between the UPIA and the trust document, the specific requirements of the trust document in question must take first priority. Where an issue is not addressed in the trust document, then the UPIA comes into play.

Uniform Principal and Income Act

Finally, we conclude the discussion of the development of the prudent investment process with the recent Uniform Principal and Income Act. Historically, separate accounting for income and principal gains has been required; thus, the accounting rules and definitions have far too often dictated the allocation decision (for example, if you wanted income you invested more in bonds because they produced "income"). This act unlinked the investment strategy from the accounting definitions for "principal" and "income." It frees the trustee to make appropriate distributions out of either pot—the central concern is to treat all beneficiaries fairly despite the technicalities of the accounting. In essence, it strongly suggests a "spending policy" based on total return, similar to what endowments have done for years. Still, the trust document takes priority over provisions in the act whenever appropriate directions are provided.

The Uniform Principal and Income Act was approved by the Uniform Laws Commission in 1997 and is slowly working its way through state legislatures.

In Summary: Ten Prudent Investment Guidelines

1. The trustee must act as a "prudent investor," using reasonable care, a high level of skill and appropriate caution.

2. Decisions are to be evaluated in the context of the portfolio as a whole, not by individual security. All possible investment

opportunities should be considered. No particular investment is inherently prudent or imprudent.

3. An overall investment strategy must align with the risk tolerance and return objectives established by trustees. Because some level of risk is unavoidable, an appropriate risk/return trade-off reasonably suited to the circumstances must be established.

4. Investment and management decisions must take all relevant factors into consideration.

5. The trustee must make a reasonable effort to ascertain and verify all relevant facts.

6. A portfolio must be diversified across and within asset classes to minimize the risk of large losses—unless not advantageous.

7. Costs must be reasonable and controlled.

8. There is a duty to monitor: the trustee has a continuing responsibility for the suitability of investments, both current and proposed.

9. Impartiality is required between the needs of current and future beneficiaries—actions and strategies must be for the benefit of all beneficiaries.

10. The trustee's duty is to the purposes, terms, distribution requirements and other circumstances of the trust, as well as applicable laws and regulations.

Document your process—put it in writing!

One of the great services we as advisors provide to our clients is not to be investment geniuses, but rather to offer a reasonable strategy and to help take away the worry and the day-to-day hassle clients feel they should attend to.

Fiduciary Investment Checklist

- Investments are managed in accordance with applicable laws, trust documents, and written Investment Policy Statements.

- Fiduciaries are aware of their duties and responsibilities.

- Fiduciaries and parties in interest are not involved with self-dealing.

- Service agreements and contracts are in writing, and do not contain provisions that conflict with fiduciary standards of care.

- There is documentation to show timing and distribution of cash flows and the payment of liabilities.

- A risk level has been identified.

- An expected, modeled return to meet investment objectives has been identified.

- An investment time horizon has been identified.

- Selected asset classes are consistent with the identified risk, return, and time horizon.

- The number of asset classes is consistent with portfolio size.

- There is detail to implement a specific investment strategy.

- IPS defines duties and responsibilities of all parties involved.

- IPS defines diversification and rebalancing guidelines.

- IPS defines due diligence criteria for selecting investment options.

- IPS defines monitoring criteria for investment options and service vendors.

- IPS defines procedures for controlling and accounting for investment expenses.

- IPS defines appropriately structured, socially responsible investment strategies.

- The investment strategy is implemented in compliance with the required level of prudence.

- Fiduciary is following applicable "safe harbor" provisions (when elected).

- Investment vehicles are appropriate for the portfolio size.

- A due diligence process is followed in selecting service providers, including the custodian.

- Periodic performance reports compare the performance of money managers against appropriate index, peer group, and IPS objectives.

- Periodic reviews are made of qualitative or organizational changes to money managers.

- Control procedures are in place to periodically review a money manager's policies for best execution, soft dollars, and proxy voting.

- Fees for investment management are consistent with agreements and the law.

- "Finder's fees," 12b-1 fees, or other forms of compensation that may have been paid for asset placement are appropriately applied, utilized, and documented.

* Source: Foundation for Fiduciary Studies, Pittsburgh, PA, 2000-2002

The Most Common Investment Mistake

While we find that most investors have made a lot of good decisions about their portfolios (they may also have made a few disastrous ones), more often than not, these have been a series of unrelated decisions that led to a "helter skelter" portfolio. Moreover, many of these decisions over the years have been driven by two emotions—Fear and Greed. Emotional decisions occur when there is no overriding plan.

One of the great services we as advisors provide to our clients is not to be investment geniuses, but rather to offer a reasonable strategy, consistently and with discipline, to help take away the worry and the day-to-day hassle clients feel they should attend to.

The Investment Process

Know Your Client

CHOOSING YOUR CLIENTS WELL is the first critical step to a successful client-advisor relationship. If you can't do what your client wants and expects (or really needs), assuming that the wants and needs are reasonable, then you will both be unhappy in the relationship. Better to clarify that earlier rather than later.

So, how do you do that? You have to get to know them. We think there are two parts to that process. First, you need to spend time asking them questions and listening to the answers. Second, you can have them bring in all their data and fill out questionnaires.

Choosing your clients well is the first critical step to a successful client-advisor relationship.

You will often get different answers from the questionnaire than you will when you talk with the client face-to-face. You therefore need to make use of both in-depth discussions and collection of hard data.

Early Interviews

For personal insight, we think the interviews are the more important. As you evaluate whether this will be a good client for you, here are some questions you might consider asking in your interviews before taking on a new client:

- What do you expect and want from me?

- If you have used other professional advisors, what has been your experience? Describe your best experiences... your worst ones.

- If we were to work together, what would need to happen over the next three years for you to be able to look back and consider hiring us to have been a successful decision?

- What do you own? What do you owe? What do you earn? What do you spend?

- How do you go about trying to save money? What has been your success in doing it?

- What has been your worst financial mistake? What did you learn from it?

- Have you ever sued a financial professional?

- What has been your best financial decision?

- What have been your memorable investment experiences?

- What worries you? What keeps you awake at night?

- If you had enough money so that it wasn't a concern, how would you live your life today?

- If you were told you were going to die tomorrow, what regrets would you have about your life?

- What's important about money to you? (See *Values Based Selling* by Bill Bachrach)

- What were your money messages as a child?

- Ask sufficient questions to learn the client's investment knowledge and expectations.

Managing Client Expectations

It's become a bit of a buzzword and therefore perhaps loses its importance, but we cannot overemphasize the importance of managing client expectations. So how do you do it?

Discuss what you can and can't do and how you do it. The client needs to know what to expect from you. Will you be picking stocks or funds or managers? Will you consult with the client before making any changes to their portfolio or take full discretion? Will you be trading often or infrequently? Do you consider their taxes or special needs? If they recommend buying or avoiding a particular stock, will you comply, and if so, how? Will you be trying to anticipate market moves, and if so, how often and on what basis?

If the clients are not aware of how you do things, then you will inevitably have misunderstandings and unnecessarily lose clients because of it. There is no reason why clients should ever be surprised. All you need to do is tell them what is reasonable for them to expect. And tell them again. And again. And again. And again. This is not their area of expertise, so they are not going to fully comprehend what you say the first or second time. We use our meetings, our newsletters, our Web site, our ADV, our marketing materials and every other opportunity to interact with clients to explain what we do and reinforce what we've told them before about our principles, our values, our processes and how we develop our recommendations, and how these relate to their personal needs and concerns.

Discuss what you can and can't do and how you do it. The client needs to know what to expect from you.

As part of managing expectations, it is equally important that you be sure you know what the client expects. Are their return expectations realistic? How involved do they want to be? Do they expect to manage the account themselves or micromanage you? Do they want to own individual stocks or are funds OK? What about active versus passive management?

Roger C. Gibson* offers a matrix about client expectations, which is an excellent tool for explaining your own philosophy and uncovering theirs:

**You Can Successfully
Time the Market**

	YES	NO
You Can Successfully Identify Stocks that will Outperform the Market — **YES**		
NO		

By each of you plotting your answers on this grid, you can quickly get a picture of where you agree and where you don't.

It is vital to the success of your practice and perhaps to your own sanity that you remember that you can't be right for everyone. Don't be afraid to refuse business. Clients who don't listen, who have philosophies different from yours, who have unrealistic expectations of the markets or of you, are virtually always more trouble than they are worth.

---

* *Asset Allocation: Balancing Financial Risk, 3rd Edition.* © 2000, 1996, 1990 by Roger C. Gibson, published by The McGraw Hill Companies.

The Questionnaire

Appendix A provides a questionnaire that we use to assess client attitudes and risk tolerances. In it we are looking for:

- Client goals and objectives

- Client fears and concerns

- Investment time frame

- Expected outside mortality
  (what age is it unlikely the client will live beyond?)

- Retirement time frame

- Shorter-term financial needs

- Risk tolerance attitudes, or how a client "feels" about

    — Negative investment performance and losing money

    — Frequent and unpredictable ups and downs of the market

    — Negative investment trends

The reason to try to measure these questions is to try to obtain a certain level of objectivity in making your judgments. If you have asked the same question in the same way to lots of people, you will begin to appreciate where in the continuum this client probably fits. Your objective is to develop a plan to fit the client, and you can't do that without an in-depth understanding of what they want, what they really need and what would cause them to deviate from the plan. It is your fiduciary responsibility to understand the client. The measurement is ultimately subjective, not objective, but the more you can standardize the process, the better judgments you'll be able to make. (See the questionnaire in Appendix A.)

Don't be afraid to refuse business. It is vital to the success of your practice and perhaps to your own sanity that you remember that you can't be right for everyone.

When advising your client, the advice needs to be given in context of their total financial picture.

You also need to get basic financial information—their balance sheet, their income and expenses and savings patterns, and a copy of their tax return. Ideally, you would also learn about their insurance coverages as well. When you are considering how to advise them on their investments, the advice needs to be given in context of their total financial picture. You need to consider not only the emotional and time frame issues described above, but you also need to understand the client's expected cash inflows and outflows and the financial capacity to take on risk.

The Nine-Step Investment Process

We believe that good and prudent investing is best done as a nine-stage process as represented by the graph on the next page. Each step will be uniquely determined based on the advisor's biases and preferences. We define Policy Issues as those that require you to make judgment determinations over predetermined form.

1. Know Why Your Client is Investing/ Identifying Goals

As we have said before, it is critical that you understand what the client wants and needs, and that there be an alignment between your understanding and the client's expectations.

Determining the Client's Goal

The differences in policy approaches here rely on the questions you ask and the information you hope to identify. At one end of the continuum, investment managers may only wish to know if the client wants to be aggressive, moderate or conservative. Alternatively, they might only wish to have the client self-identify as wanting growth, income or a balance. At the other end of the continuum is the financial planning model in which we seek to know

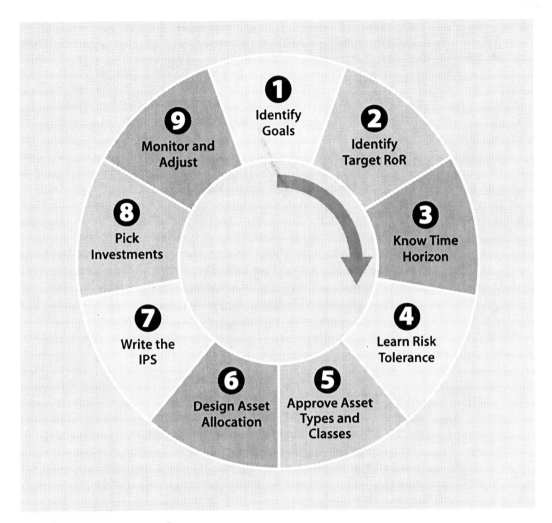

The Nine-Step Investment Process

about a client's values and life goals/wishes, and how the rest of their financial and personal life supports or doesn't support these desires. It is our bias that the more you know about a client, the more insight you'll have about how to be of service and how to design an investment program that best addresses all their needs. Keep in mind, clients who have not allowed themselves to spend a lot of time thinking about what they want out of life may not have

For individual clients, we think the determination about the needed rate of return is the driving factor in determining the appropriate asset allocation.

clear answers to your questions initially, or they may even provide a misleading picture; it is generally necessary to probe multiple times in different ways to successfully elicit a true understanding. Also, keep in mind that over time the client's goals and risk tolerance may change, so it is necessary to check back in periodically to make sure that your earlier assumptions and understandings remain accurate.

2. Identify a Target or Needed Rate of Return

We believe that the need for return should drive much of the remainder of the design process. If the client has as much as they'll ever need or want, they don't need to take unnecessary investment risks; as a result, a very conservative investment approach may be most appropriate. However, if they are going to be a little short in reaching their goals, ratcheting up the risk of the portfolio to more likely achieve the needed higher returns may be the best answer. But if all they need is a six percent return, why go for extra returns and give them a portfolio that exposes them to unnecessary risk?

For individual clients, we think the determination about the needed rate of return is the driving factor in determining the appropriate asset allocation. If a client needs nine percent returns for the rest of their life to be reasonably certain of not running out of money before death and still satisfying their life goals and dreams, then in our view that fact becomes more important than their risk tolerance. Obviously you can't ignore the risk tolerance issue, but it is subject to change, given a lot of education and given an in-depth discussion of the trade-offs the client may have to make.

In fact, we would go so far as to say that if you accept the assignment of helping a client with a portfolio and you determine they need a nine percent return to achieve their future personal goals, but find that they will only tolerate the risk that comes with a lower returning portfolio, then you bear some responsibility when they eventually run out of money.

If neither goal adjustment nor education helps bring the portfolio design into an acceptable risk/return relationship, then we would recommend resigning from the account. If you have a pretty good idea the plan will be inadequate and yet you go ahead with it (probably because you need the income), then we think it very likely that you'll eventually share a professional and perhaps financial obligation when your plan fails.

Capital Needs Analysis— So What Rate of Return Do I Need?

Your plan is predicated on your knowing what rate of return is needed by the client to allow them to attain their goals and not run out of money. To know that, you need to do a retirement projection, or what we call a "capital needs analysis." In effect, you need to measure the projected inflows and outflows of the client's financial existence through the year when it is virtually no longer possible that they will be alive. Obviously, this is an inexact science. Investment returns will vary. Inflation will vary. There may be an unexpected windfall or expense. They may work longer or get sick and need medical care.

All that being said, you have to start somewhere. You need to work with the client to make the best guess possible about what will happen in their future. Then you need to solve for an investment rate of return that will have the best chance of success in ensuring they will not run out of money before death. Almost every planning software available has some form of a capital needs analysis. One of the most complete is that available from Money Tree Software, called "Golden Years" software. Many planners have also developed their own proprietary spreadsheets, as we have.

Dealing with the variables is difficult at best. It used to be that planners would use their spreadsheets and then use conservative and likely sets of inputs, and this created some sense of the sensitivity and downside risk for each set of assumptions. More recently, Monte Carlo simulations have been used to measure the

Your plan is predicated on your knowing what rate of return is needed by the client to allow them to attain their goals and not run out of money.

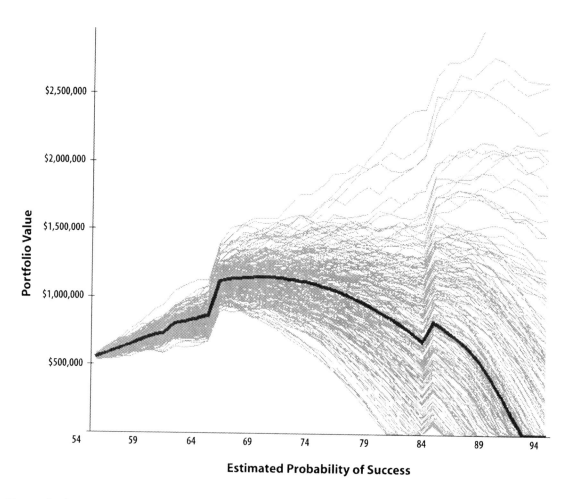

Monte Carlo Output from "Golden Years" Software

uncertainty. Monte Carlo allows the planner to identify the variables and then to determine a range and pattern for what those variables might be. Then by running the calculations 100, 1,000, or 10,000 times and having the computer randomly select the variables within the pattern, the calculation results can indicate the probabilities of the possible outcomes—both the range of what is possible and the frequency of each.

While this might seem overly complicated, clients intuitively understand that their lives do not operate in straight lines. They also understand probabilities ("There's a 40 percent chance of showers today in the city"). Therefore, after explaining the variables and the assumptions, clients will understand when you inform them that based on that input (remember: "garbage in, garbage out"), you've determined that they have an 82 percent chance of both attaining their financial goals and not running out of money before they die.

When the capital needs analysis is completed, you should have a pretty good idea of what rate of investment return the client needs.

3. Understand the Time Horizon

If the client plans on making purchases or withdrawals in the near future, then the time horizon may be limited for at least part of the portfolio and the design should be adjusted accordingly. If the investment time horizon is a decade or longer, then the client will have more freedom to take risks and allow time to balance out bad years with other good years.

What Time Horizon Do You Use?

Let's say your client is a trust and the funds will be distributed to the remaindermen beneficiaries every so often in the future. Will the transference of ownership be in cash or in some in-kind portion of the invested assets? The answer may make a difference as to how you invest those dollars as the transfer date approaches.

Or let's say college expenses are coming up in a few years or the client wants to buy a home or retirement is only five years away. What policies will you use for investing the funds for those short time horizons?

College expenses don't come all at once. They normally are spread over four or more years, and each of the years can be split up into months, quarters or semesters. Therefore, the same decision doesn't necessarily need to be made for all the funds reserved for that purpose. Perhaps a year (or two or three) ahead of when

For most individuals, retirement is not synonymous with the end of life. It therefore does not make sense to completely change an investment philosophy solely as a result of retirement.

the funds are needed, you pull the needed amount of money out of the market. Do you put it in cash or in a somewhat higher yielding instrument designed to mature when it is needed?

The goal of buying a house is not necessarily as time dependent as funding a college education. So, it may be OK to keep invested funds intended for the purchase until the client is ready to buy, with the idea of maximizing the value. If the market falls, then the client can simply continue to rent or do without that second home for a while until the market comes back. Or if the client is set on the purchase date and you have to create the reserve, you'll need to decide where to keep it and how to handle it.

If the client is a company, is the business likely to end when the owner retires? If so, retirement may have definite implications for how the portfolio is managed in the few years before that date.

For most individuals, retirement is not synonymous with the end of life. It therefore does not make sense to completely change an investment philosophy solely as a result of retirement, assuming the client expects to live for some time after that date. But it may make sense to change a few things. The financial change at retirement is that the employment income stops and new sources of income are needed to replace it. A client's investments or other sources may be needed to pay them a substitute salary. So at retirement, you may need to create a reserve that was not previously appropriate. Most of the rest of the assets will likely continue to be fully invested, since they will be needed to grow over the next 30 years or so. You may also need to start a process of "reverse dollar-cost averaging" in which you sell off small amounts of the portfolio at a time periodically to provide an income over the remainder of the client's projected life.

It's also possible that the client's risk tolerance changes at retirement as a result of not earning further income, and so the portfolio design may need to also change. But make sure that a new capital needs analysis is calculated to see if the projections work successfully with a less aggressive investment posture.

4. Understand Risk and Your Client's Tolerance for It

For institutional clients, the degree of risk deemed acceptable will be a primary driver for what level of returns can be obtained and what the portfolio will therefore look like. For individual clients, we think risk tolerance is more of an education issue, because if they need nine percent to attain their goals, they are probably going to need to accept the risk that comes with it (or adjust their goals).

Measuring Risk Tolerance

In assessing risk tolerance, ultimately, you are trying to ascertain the client's "Maalox moment," the point at which the client will panic or ask to sell out of a difficult market. What degree of decline will cause the client to simply refuse to stay invested in stocks, or for that matter, bonds? We know most investors' greatest difficulty is staying in the game when the going gets tough, and those who sell in panic or disgust are simply creating real losses out of possible losses. It is a point every advisor wants to help clients avoid. The point is different for different people, and therefore requires some expertise to be able to identify the most likely point. Once you think you have it, you can design a portfolio so that in almost all circumstances (95 percent or even 99 percent confidence level), the portfolio is unlikely to go down that far.

Getting a sense of a client's willingness to tolerate risk is critical to finding the right portfolio design. How you make this determination and how you use that information in designing the portfolio need to be recorded as part of the Investment Policy Statement. The client owns his or her own investment policy. Therefore, the more clearly you describe what the client was thinking at the time and how that was used to establish the investment approach could be important as a historical record should there be a later disagreement. It can protect the advisor if the client has signed off on (agreed to) a description of their willingness to accept risk in understandable language and a clear description of how that conclusion was reached.

For institutional clients, the degree of risk deemed acceptable will be a primary driver for what the portfolio will therefore look like.

What instrument was used to bring you to a conclusion about the client's tolerance for risk? Is it thorough? Well thought-out? Does it have any basis in scientific research?

We have included a copy of the risk tolerance and investment policy questionnaire we use both in Appendix A.

Measuring Risk Capacity

When we are trying to understand a client's financial ability to accept risk ("financial capacity"), what we really want to know is: How much risk can they afford to take? To measure this, we need to look at:

- **Age and Life Expectancy**—what's their real time horizon?

- **Income (Stability and Amount) versus Spending**—just because their income is high doesn't mean they can take on lots of risk. The first rule of financial planning is to spend less than you make.

- **Liquidity**—relative to their net worth and to the risks you are proposing, what kind of cash reserves do they have on hand?

- **Net Worth**—relative to the size of the portfolio.

- **Debt and Debt Service**—look at both the relative size and the fixed versus flexible nature of the payments.

- **Insurance**—insurance is intended to cover what would otherwise be financial disasters or difficulties. How well are they covered for life? Disability? Medical? Property and casualty?

- **Family Responsibilities**—to what extent are others depending on the client's ability to provide and how well are they covered?

As you look at these questions, you'll probably realize that effective planning can help improve the client's capacity to take on risk. As you work with a client and improve their "scoring" on these factors, they'll be able to afford to take more risk, and hopefully receive the rewards that come with it.

You'll note that we have differentiated "risk tolerance" from "risk capacity." This was based on some excellent work by Rick Adkins of The Arkansas Financial Group of Little Rock, Arkansas. According to Adkins,

"Risk tolerance" is the emotional and intellectual ability to withstand volatility and a given degree of loss.

"Risk capacity" is the financial ability to withstand volatility or loss.

The latter may not be consistent with the client's emotional or subjective risk tolerance. Both factors are important in the determinations you will make regarding the structure and implementation of the client's portfolio.

Problems with Assessing Risk Tolerance

It's important to be aware of some of the problems in trying to come to a clear understanding of a client's risk tolerance. First and foremost, clients often do not know their own risk tolerance, so their answers to such questions often do not reflect a true picture.

They often suffer from "recency bias" in which their recent experience overshadows longer-term experience. When markets have been good for a while, investors tend to believe they can tolerate more risk than might otherwise be true. When the markets have been tough, investors often shy away from what might normally be considered a reasonable amount of risk for their circumstances.

Clients' investment preferences or fears can be irrational. Perhaps a recent experience or one in early childhood created an illogical fear. Perhaps they have heard and believed all the media attention to short-term volatility. Perhaps they just don't know much about the markets and how they work—most of us fear what we don't know. Regardless of the reason for the fear, risk tolerance tends to change as clients become more educated, as they better understand the process, the objectives and the real risks. Education is therefore an important part of what advisors can do for clients.

5. Identify Acceptable Investment Categories and Vehicles

Before you can develop an asset allocation, you need to identify what kinds of investments your client is willing to own and not own. There may be other issues that will influence the decisions you need to make about what assets to hold or buy or how the allocation needs to be balanced for or against a particular segment.

At the broadest level, you have to decide on the asset classes. For most investors, stocks, bonds and cash equivalents are easy. But you also need to look at the sub-classes because some of them may not be acceptable. Among equities, you may need to examine which of the following will be acceptable to the client:

- Large U.S. stocks—growth and value

- Small U.S. stocks—growth and value

- International stocks—large and small, growth and value

- Emerging markets

- Real estate investment trusts

- Sectors

You need to ask similar questions about bonds: Which of the following will be acceptable?

- Government bonds

- Investment quality corporate bonds

- High-yield bonds

- Tax-free municipal bonds

- Mortgage bonds

- CMOs (Collateralized Mortgage Obligations)

- Government-backed foreign bonds

- Emerging market bonds

- Others you may recommend

What about other assets and asset classes? For example:

- Real estate (direct and indirect)

- Venture capital

- Hedge funds

- Other alternative investments

- Business assets

You also need to examine what form of the investment is or is not acceptable. For example, you should get agreement ahead of time regarding the use of any of the following, or similar:

- Individual stocks or bonds

- Mutual funds (open, closed, exchange traded)

- Limited or other partnerships

- Managed or separate accounts

Other investment issues that may need to be clarified before the asset allocation is established include:

- Socially responsible issues—it will be important to understand what kinds of companies and investments the client wants to avoid or support. Then you will have to decide whether you can deliver what is wanted.

- Concentrated stock positions or existing positions that are, or are not, going to be liquidated. If you hold them in the overall portfolio and as part of the asset allocation, the lack of diversification may positively or negatively affect your performance and the volatility of the portfolio. Is there a liquidation policy (moving toward improved diversification)? If so, it should be clear what the client expects and what you will provide. If you are simply holding these assets, will you charge a full fee, even though you really can't manage the assets? Will you keep this one (or more) stock(s) outside of the asset allocation design? If so, would it be better in a different, nonmanaged and perhaps not-billed account?

- Sometimes the client has other advisors working with parts of the total portfolio and it may be important to be aware of what decisions are being made or what assets are being held elsewhere. That being said, we caution against agreeing to mold your portfolio around the other advisor's ideas. Doing so could subject your managed portfolio to periods of substantially greater volatility or relative underperformance, thus putting you at a possible competitive disadvantage.

6. Establish an Acceptable Allocation of Asset Categories

Developing the Portfolio Allocation

At this point in the process, you should have a good knowledge of your client and what they want from their investments. The next step is to design the asset allocation, or how the portfolio will be divided among stocks, bonds and cash, between large and small companies, between U.S. and foreign companies, between value and growth, between taxable and tax-free bonds, between growth and income, and in what proportions.

In our view, asset allocation is the crucial investment decision. According to a famous study published in the May 1991 *Financial Analysts Journal* by Brinson, Singer and Beebower and later updated by Brinson, Hood and Beebower, roughly 90 percent of the variability in returns among the pension funds studied was the result of asset allocation decisions. The remaining ten percent came from what most people assume is more responsible for returns: securities

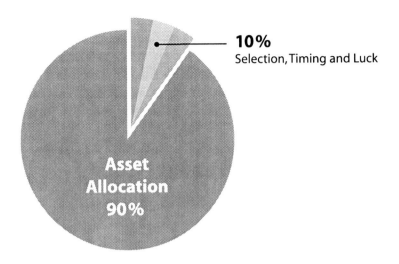

10%
Selection, Timing and Luck

Asset Allocation 90%

Getting the right asset allocation is a critical step in the successful investment process.

selection, timing of market movements and random luck. Therefore, getting the right asset allocation is a critical step in the successful investment process.

Diversification versus Asset Allocation

Sometimes the terms "diversification" and "asset allocation" are confused. While they are similar in concept, there are some important differences. Asset allocation takes it to a higher level.

Diversification generally means "Don't put all your eggs in one basket." At the lowest level, if you like auto stocks, diversifying would mean owning GM, Ford and Daimler-Chrysler instead of just one of them. But, in all probability, if one is dropping in price, then probably so are the others because most of the economic influences on one are the same as on the others in this group. On the other hand, if you owned GM, Merck, HP and Disney, there would be fewer cross-over influences since these companies are in very different industries, so it would be more likely that if one were going down, not all of them would be doing so.

Asset allocation, on the other hand, uses many baskets of many designs and does so in purposeful proportions. For example, an asset allocation (portfolio design) might include all of the following: large and small U.S. stocks, foreign stocks, U.S. and foreign bonds, and real estate. Note that these are each broader asset classes rather than individual companies or industries. The overall portfolio design (proportional assignments), and the concern with asset classes and their respective risk and return and volatility correlations, are what distinguish asset allocation from simple diversification.

7. Write the Investment Policy Statement

With the understanding you have developed about the client and how the client wishes to have their money invested, it's now time to write it down, share it with the client and have the client sign off, indicating approval. See sample templates in Appendix B.

8. Pick the Specific Investments that Fit the Allocation Model

Once you know how much is going to go into small cap value or large cap foreign or tax-free municipal bonds (from step 6), then you can select the specific securities to be utilized in the portfolio.

Since there are lots of available resources on how to pick the "right" investment, we won't spend further time here on this issue.

9. Monitor and Adjust as Appropriate

Investment management is an ongoing process that must adapt as money is added to or withdrawn from the portfolio, as values change, as the economy and markets change, as managers leave, etc. Perhaps most importantly, portfolio changes may become necessary when important changes happen in your client's circumstances. The ongoing process involves a number of decisions and moving parts:

Rebalancing

Rebalancing is a way of keeping the risk/reward profile of a portfolio relatively constant. As a by-product, in a portfolio without significant additions or withdrawals, it also systematizes and provides a discipline in the process of buying low and selling high. This occurs because as portfolio values fluctuate, with gaining asset classes growing above their target allocations and losing asset classes shrinking below their targets, the portfolio will look less and less like the originally agreed-upon allocation. Since that original design reflected the desired return characteristics and acceptable risk levels, it is important to maintain a discipline that more or less retains those same characteristics.

Assuming consistency is desirable, as segments of the portfolio move out of targeted alignment, it is important to periodically bring them back into alignment. The parts that get sold off are those parts that have gained in proportion to the other parts ("selling high") and the parts that get purchased or added to are those parts that have lost ground in relation to the other portfolio parts ("buying low"). Rebalancing therefore provides a discipline to keep the portfolio in balance or true to its agreed-upon risk and return parameters, and by systematically buying low and selling high, overall portfolio returns will often be enhanced.

For example, if you start with a portfolio design that calls for 25 percent in large U.S. stocks, and after a while the market changes have moved that to 33 percent of the portfolio, what, if anything, do you do about that? Rebalancing may or may not be something you do as an investment manager. We think it should be. If it is, you should describe the process in the IPS.

Investment Selection Changes

Unless you are running an entirely passive portfolio (using index-based vehicles for each part of your portfolio, so that there are never any decisions being made about what stocks or bonds or managers are worthy of being added to or subtracted from the

Rebalancing provides a discipline to keep the portfolio in balance or true to its agreed-upon risk and return parameters, and by systematically buying low and selling high, overall portfolio returns will often be enhanced.

The more you can document your procedures and thought process in the IPS, the easier the relationship will be.

portfolio), then you will need to periodically make changes as managers or funds move into or out of favor.

We suggest that you have a system or a process for making your decisions. Remember, it is important for the client to be able to understand what you are doing for them and why you are doing it. If you make a new recommendation or if they see a change happen in a discretionary portfolio, they may want to know why. To retain the highest level of client confidence in you, you need to be able to provide a clear and consistent answer to that question. Assuming you have one, we advise writing it down. If you don't have one, we advise that you develop one. Either way, it ought to be included in your IPS.

Reporting

How often will you be reporting to your clients? What information will they get from you or from the custodian directly? Will you provide instructions as to how to read the reports or to understand the key information within them? How often will you meet with the client to discuss their portfolio (and their own circumstances, in case the portfolio needs to be changed)? Will the performance be shown after fees? What benchmarks will you use to help them analyze your investment management performance? Are there any special reporting items the client requests?

Allocation Changes

There may be times when a tactical or strategic change to the asset allocation is appropriate. Part of that will depend on your own philosophy about investing. For example, if you change your approach and now want to include hedge funds in a client's portfolio, that would require a change in the agreed-to allocation. Alternatively, if you believe making tactical moves part of your role as an advisor, then you may be making relatively frequent changes to increase or decrease a particular asset class to try to take advantage of the anticipated market environment. There are also things that happen in the lives of our clients—retirement, illness, injury, marriage, and so on—that call for a strategic re-design of the allocation.

Each of these changes should follow some sort of agreed-upon procedure. When do you need the client's approval? If you act alone, what responsibility do you have for informing the client? What triggers will be used to indicate which tactical changes are called for and will there be pre-arranged parameters within which such changes can be freely made? It is not our role to tell you how to manage the client's money, but only to point out that the more you can document your procedures and thought process in the IPS, the easier the relationship will be.

Returning to the Beginning

Keep in mind that our nine-step process is in the form of a circle. Periodically, it is critical to return to Step One and start again, to make sure that what you decided yesterday continues to serve your client well today and into tomorrow.

Difficult Policy Issues

A N INVESTMENT POLICY STATEMENT reflects the results of a discussion between advisor and client about each of the essential policies to be utilized by the advisor. Some of these policies reflect the basic style or philosophy of the advisor. It may even be why the client is hiring the advisor. Some of the policies reflect choices that get made by the advisor or the client to reflect the client's unique set of desires and circumstances. Different advisors have made different choices about each of these issues. As a result, clients are easily confused about the "right choice." It can't hurt to write it down and it is often very helpful. It does require an advisor to be very conscious about the choices being made

It is critical that the advisor understands what the client wants and needs.

and to be intentional about their investment process. As a result, there is no such thing as a "boilerplate" IPS; it needs to be different for each advisor and probably for each client. We believe this is a good thing.

Each of the issues deserves discussion, and the agreements between client and advisor should be documented so that there is a record of those agreements and the reasoning behind each of them. This is the essence of an Investment Policy Statement— a review of each of the issues and the agreements that have been determined. If there is any possibility of future misunderstanding, no issue is too small. Documenting the agreements can be helpful simply to clarify and communicate them and in protecting the advisor (for doing what was agreed) should the client disagree later.

One way to organize these policy issues is to think about the investment process. We have organized this chapter into the nine steps of the investment process, as we see it. Each step along the way raises a new set of issues.

The Difficult Issues in Each Step

Step 1: Identify Goals

The Depth of Understanding

How much time and effort do you put into learning about your client—their goals, their values, their needs, their fears and concerns? Some spend several meetings, long questionnaires and many hours of discussion. Some simply want to know how aggressive or conservative a client wants to be. Most probably fit somewhere in the middle. Where do you fit on this continuum? We think that the better you know a client, the better your advice will serve that client's needs.

Cash-Flow Issues

What current cash-flow requirements does the client have and what implications will this have for portfolio construction? Each conclusion represents a policy choice that should be documented in the IPS. For example, if the client's personal income is unsteady or uncertain (e.g., income derived from periodic commissions or bonuses), that client may need to set aside more in cash reserves than a salaried client.

If the client has periodic opportunities to make investments outside of their portfolio, such as real estate or private business ventures, larger reserves are probably desirable.

If the client needs to make regular withdrawals, there are several ways to address this issue. For instance, an advisor could periodically draw down from the portfolio in regular increments, either from the dividends and interest the portfolio generates. Alternatively, the advisor could sell appreciated assets or principal, as appropriate, to provide the cash needed. A second approach would be to set aside a reservoir of cash in a money market account, draw down a predetermined monthly amount, and periodically replenish the money market account with portfolio interest, dividends and capital gain distributions and investment sales to keep the account at the desired level. The determination of how much to set aside as a reservoir should be discussed with the client, as well as issues such as whether it should be in a separate account, and if so, whether management fees will be charged for this account.

Cash Balances

How much cash (money market asset class) should you design in the portfolio? What is the use for the cash? Clients need cash (checking or money market accounts) to pay for normal living expenses. The operational aspect of managing a portfolio (e.g., ease of trading, cash available to pay the management fee, etc.) requires having some cash in the portfolio. Clients may also need an emergency reserve. Decisions about the the amount of cash will

You have a professional obligation to ensure that the expected investment returns will satisfy the client's goals and that the accompanying portfolio volatility is within the client's tolerance for risk.

be influenced, not only by the topics addressed above, but will also depend on a variety of factors having to do with such things as size, consistency and future dependability of their income, other liquidity available, and borrowing resources. Each of these questions and circumstances require a policy decision.

Step 2: Identify the Target Rate of Return

The required rate of return which a client will need in order to attain his or her lifetime's financial goals should drive much of the design process. Determination of the target rate of return can be done *only* after you have performed a capital needs analysis. In effect, you need to measure the projected inflows and outflows of the client's financial existence, (based on their goals), through an extended life expectancy, such as to age 100.

Some policy issues here involve your methodology for determining this number. Have you developed your own spreadsheets, or do you use a prepackaged program? Do you use the additional aid of Monte Carlo simulation, and if so, what are the variables in those sets of calculations (e.g., standard deviations)? The advisor's choices about these questions will, in part, determine the answer to what rate of return is to be targeted.

What the client tells you should not suffice in identifying a return objective. You have a professional obligation to ensure that the expected investment returns will satisfy the client's goals *and* that the accompanying portfolio volatility is within the client's tolerance for risk. Meeting this obligation requires you to do some analysis. If the returns and risk are not aligned with an ability to satisfy the goals, then something has to give. The advisor has to spend some time educating the client about the conflict and the implications, and perhaps in finding necessary compromises.

If you determine that the investment plan will be inadequate for the client's long-term needs and yet you implement the plan as is, then you will be doing the client a disservice and may have failed to satisfy your professional obligations. Who knows—in the litigious environment we live in, you may also face negligence issues in court when your plan inevitably fails. The question is: what do you do when the client's goals or risk tolerances are unrealistic or incompatible?

Step 3: Know the Time Horizon

Some of the policy issues pertaining to time horizon include how to handle short-term and longer-term liquidity needs. For example, if a portion of the investment portfolio will be used for college expenses for undergraduate and graduate years, at what point do you begin moving the annual tuition expenses into cash? Would it make a difference if an adequate line of credit were available to the client?

How do you estimate your client's life expectancy? To measure lifetime capital-needs sufficiency, you need to estimate a mortality age. How do you choose a mortality age? Keep in mind that IRS and life insurance tables generally a use median age of death for the addressed group. Using those tables means that there is roughly a 50 percent chance of outliving the identified mortality. By themselves, these tables may not be good guides for choosing the mortality to be used in a capital needs analysis.

Often a client believes that their investment allocation should be significantly altered when they reach retirement age. How will you handle this? If they retire at age 65 and live until 95, there is still a 30-year time horizon at retirement. How conservative can the client afford to be?

If the investment portfolio being considered under the IPS is a qualified retirement plan and the owner-client is planning to retire within 2–5 years, the portfolio might have to be liquidated in order to raise cash to pay out the rollover amount or distribute to employees. Will you have a systematic approach to selling and moving into cash, or will you "roll the dice" and stay fully invested until the last minute? If there are employees participating in the plan, how do you take their potential cash distribution needs into consideration?

To measure lifetime capital-needs sufficiency, you need to estimate a mortality age.

Step 4: Understand Your Client's Risk Tolerance

Getting a sense of a client's willingness to tolerate risk is critical to finding the right portfolio design so that the client will stay true to the course during both good and difficult times. How you make this determination and how you use that information in designing the portfolio need to be recorded as part of the Investment Policy Statement. The client owns (and will be living emotionally) with his or her own investment policy. Therefore, how clearly you describe what the client was thinking at the time, and how that was used to establish the investment approach, could be important as a historical record should there be a later disagreement.

For institutional clients, the degree of risk deemed acceptable will be a primary driver for what level of returns can be obtained and how the portfolio will be structured. For individual clients, we think risk tolerance is more of an education issue, because if they need to achieve a high return to attain their goals, they are probably going to need to accept the risk that comes with it (or adjust their goals).

What instrument or questionnaire was used to arrive at your conclusion about the client's tolerance for risk? Is it thorough? Well thought-out? Does it have any basis in scientific research?

As discussed in chapter 3, we think there is a difference between "risk tolerance" and "risk capacity." Just because someone can emotionally stomach the ups and downs of the market doesn't mean they are a good candidate for fully participating in those risks. If they have dependent children, little insurance, no net worth or high expenses and a volatile income stream, high-risk investing may be inappropriate, regardless of their emotional tolerance for risk. In this case, "the weakest link" is generally the determining factor for how much risk an investor can accept. If the capacity to take on risk is the limiting factor, then as these factors strengthen, the client should be able to take on more risk. In all likelihood, such an investor will need the higher returns that are offered by the greater risk.

Does the process you are using to determine your recommendations allow you to learn about a client's capacity to take on risk? Do you think you do a good job of really learning about a client's emotional tolerance for market volatility? If not, then perhaps you need to review your process and be more thorough about how you gain an understanding of your client.

Step 5: Identify Asset Classes and Investment Vehicles

Addressing Concentrated Positions

Besides the basic identification of the asset classes, how do you handle a portfolio with a concentration of a single stock, or investment sector? Possibly your client has one or more securities that they don't want to sell for tax or purely emotional or non-logical reasons. Or maybe they have 60 percent of their assets in one stock. You need to develop policies for how you are going to deal with these situations. Maybe you dollar-cost-average out of these positions and if so, over what time frame? How often? Will there be triggers to cause you to do more or less? Maybe you simply hold these positions and work around them. Do you treat the rest of the portfolio as though those positions didn't exist, or do you let them affect what you do with the rest of the portfolio?

For example, let's say a client comes to you with an outsized position (50 percent of their investment wealth) in General Electric stock. If they want to continue to hold GE, what are the implications for the rest of the portfolio?

Do you assume that GE is a proxy for the U.S. stock market, which might mean it would be the only U.S. stock you hold?

Perhaps you think it is a good proxy, but only for large U.S. stocks, so you might include small U.S. stocks as an asset class in the other half of the portfolio, as well as foreign stocks, real estate, cash and/or bonds.

Perhaps you think that it is not a good proxy, but it does certainly represent an important part of the Dow Jones Industrial Average and the Standard & Poor's 500 Stock Index.

With that in mind, you might choose to divide the remaining half of the portfolio not only with small U.S. stocks, foreign stocks, real estate, cash and/or bonds, but also with some other large U.S. stocks. Or you might consider the GE to be so concentrated and therefore so nonrepresentative that you build a portfolio design for half of the portfolio as though the GE didn't exist. There's not a right or wrong way to approach these kinds of issues. It is important to acknowledge the many ways to deal with it, present your philosophy about the issues, seek the client's guidance and concurrance, and then come up with an approach that works for each of you and is operationally practical.

Investment Style

Are you a proponent of passively managed vehicles such as index funds or exchange traded index funds (ETFs), and if so, for all or only a few asset classes?

Do you have a bias toward value over growth? What if the client refuses to own a particular asset class that you believe is imperative to be included? How is this documented?

Does the client wish to invest only in "socially conscious" investments and if so, what is their definition of socially conscious?

Designating Asset Classes

Some advisors focus their recommendations on the specific investments they think their client should own. While this is important, we believe it is more logical and ultimately more important to first determine which asset classes are to be included in the portfolio (and which are not to be included) and then how the portfolio "pie" is to be proportioned among them. Starting with the Big Picture gives the client a framework for understanding the subsequent specific investment recommendations.

Do you expect to be investing all of a client's money, or just a portion? If the latter, then you may be able to focus on just one element of a total portfolio, and everyone should be absolutely clear which element that will be and how it is defined. If you are dealing with the more complete picture, then you'll probably want to have investments in several categories.

What is an asset class? We could call "equities" an asset class, or we could begin to assign qualifiers—U.S. stocks, small company U.S. equities, small growth U.S. equities, or even small growth technology U.S. companies. None of these is "right" or "wrong." However you define your asset classes, the client has a right to know your approach and how you will be investing their dollars. To avoid later misunderstandings and to appropriately manage client expectations, having a discussion about your approach and your style of investing can make a notable difference.

The advisor should discuss the approach to be used, get the client's agreement and then document the approach in the IPS.

Step 6: Design the Asset Allocation

Tax Considerations

The client's portfolio must be designed with the client's tax status in mind.

One of the important questions is choosing where to put different assets and what format the assets will take. For taxable accounts, it may be desirable to minimize both current income and turnover (thus lowering annual taxable capital gains). For tax-deferred accounts, it may be an attractive option to try to do almost precisely the opposite—place the income-producing investments here and give more credit to maximizing pre-tax returns. Is the investor better off if the faster-growing assets are placed in the tax-deferred accounts to take fullest advantage of the compounding opportunities or in the taxable account to take advantage of lower capital gains rates?

Will you attempt to regularly harvest tax losses or leave those decisions to another professional such as the client's accountant?

Low-Basis Securities

If a client is quite elderly and has many low-basis investments in their portfolio, the advisor should take into consideration that sell-

How do know if you have developed an optimal asset allocation if you don't use an optimizer?

ing at the start of the management relationship or any time thereafter simply to reallocate a portfolio may deny the heirs a step-up in basis. If this is an issue, how you plan to address it? These types of discussions are what add value to your client relationship.

Portfolio Organization

Some advisors believe in a "core and satellite" approach to investing to help save taxes. Whether you use this or your own approach, it is appropriate to describe the situation and the issues and any policies that will be followed as a result.

Optimization

How do know if you have developed an optimal asset allocation if you don't use an optimizer? It is imperative if you present an asset allocation that you identify the source and the variables used in developing the recommendation. If you have obtained an asset allocation from your broker-dealer or insurance company or bank, we strongly suggest that you find out how it was developed and the assumptions used in its development.

Are you going to identify a specific and static percentage for each asset class in the portfolio or are you going to identify an acceptable range of percentages for that asset class? For example, if your allocation has the U.S. Large Cap with 40 percent of the total portfolio, will it be allowed to fluctuate between 30 percent and 50 percent or do you want to try to keep it more consistent? This policy decision will have further ramifications for the rebalancing process.

Dealing with Other Accounts

Often, clients like to have their own "play account" in which they invest on the basis of their own whims or "helpful hints" from others. They may have other brokerage accounts, or Uniform Transfer to Minors Act (UTMA) account or other specific-purpose accounts. To what extent will the existence of these assets affect the decisions made for this portfolio?

How will other assets owned by the client be handled vis-à-vis the decisions being made about this portfolio? Sometimes the client has other advisors working with parts of the total portfolio, and it may be important to be aware of what decisions are being made or what assets are being held by those advisors. That being said, we caution against agreeing to mold your portfolio around some other advisor's ideas. Doing so could subject your managed portfolio to periods of substantially greater volatility or relative underperformance, thus putting you at a possible competitive disadvantage, and the client's overall wealth could be adversely affected by its being managed in an information vacuum or without a unifying Big Picture.

Often clients have a small account held for the benefit of a child (for example, a Uniform Transfer to Minors Act account). These can be problematic as part of a larger portfolio. Each such account should be prudently managed and should probably be invested to stand on its own. That implies its own asset allocation, and perhaps its own IPS. At the same time, it is ultimately part of a family's total portfolio and therefore perhaps should be addressed as part of that greater portfolio. Another possibility is to not accept accounts with less than some specified amount, but what does the investor then do with the UTMA account, or similar small, stand-alone accounts?

Do you have the identical asset allocation for each spouse's assets if they both have the same risk tolerance but all of the husband's assets are in a retirement plan? What if one client has a different risk tolerance than the co-client? Do you develop a separate IPS for each one? What if that retirement plan doesn't offer the complete range of investment choices you recommend in your investment policy? Are you going to recommend an asset allocation specifically for the retirement plan and if so, what responsibilities do you have to monitor changes in managers and values?

Step 7: Write the Investment Policy Statement

The final two steps in the investment process—selecting the investments and then managing the portfolio—necessarily arise after the IPS is written. These are the implementation steps and by definition should be directed by the Investment Policy Statement.

Step 8: Select the Investments

You have already identified the asset classes and types of investment vehicles to be included in the portfolio and now the next step is what the client normally believes is the most important part of the process—investment selection. As most of us have come to believe, selection of specific securities is relatively less important than the asset allocation decision, but an IPS should still have documented your selection process.

The most important policy decision in this part of the process is, are you going to delegate the selection of the specific managers, mutual funds or stocks to a third party, or are you going to select the individual securities yourself? If you are delegating the selection of specific funds or managers to a third party, how have you selected this third party? If you are selecting the investments yourself, what are your criteria? The client has a right to understand your process methodology.

If you have decided to employ a passive approach to investment management, will you use mutual funds or exchange traded funds, or some other approach, and why?

If you are selecting funds, should you use those that have no commissions or transaction fees assessed by the custodian, or does that make a difference? We might suggest that if a client is systematically depositing or withdrawing funds, then "no transaction fee" investments may be most cost effective and appropriate. If transactions are seldom anticipated, then paying a small transaction charge for a low expense fund may be better for the client.

Amount of Discretion

Part of the understanding between the advisor and the client involves the extent to which the advisor makes all the decisions ("full discretion") or to which the client has rights to be consulted and change the recommended tactic prior to the recommendation being executed. There's no right or wrong way to do things, but the client has a right to know your procedure.

Other Advisors or Decision Influencers

Accountants, attorneys, trust officers, trustees and others may have an interest in and influence over some or much of what goes into the investment policy development. Where this situation exists, it may be helpful to identify who they are and what their role might be. For example, who gets a copy of the IPS? Do they need to be informed about investment changes or recommendations? Before the fact or just as a courtesy?

Step 9: Monitoring, Managing and Reporting

Rebalancing

Do you intend to rebalance the portfolio or will a buy-and-hold strategy be employed? If you plan to rebalance, will you choose an absolute or conditional rebalancing approach?

An absolute approach could include a fixed percentage variance around the policy target. For example, if the variance percentage is 5 percent, and if a particular asset class' policy target is 40 percent of the portfolio, rebalancing would occur should the actual percentage fall below 35 percent or rise above 45 percent of the total.

A conditional rebalancing approach might occur when the asset class moved 25 percent from its target. Using the 40 percent policy target, the rebalancing would occur if this asset class dropped below 30 percent or rose above 50 percent.

- Will you employ a different rebalancing approach in taxable accounts than in tax-deferred accounts?

- Will you treat extremely volatile asset classes any differently from more stable ones?

- What market or economic forces could cause a change in the rebalancing policies, if any?

- How frequently will the portfolio be reviewed for rebalancing? Will it be done on time-based frequency such as monthly, quarterly, semi-annually? Or whenever the portfolio moves out of policy ranges? Unfortunately many portfolio management reporting systems do not have the capability of notifying you when a portfolio is out of acceptable range.

Benchmarks

Which benchmarks are you going to use—pure indices that have no management or transaction fees, or category returns for managed asset classes that will reflect these costs? If you select indices, will they be capitalization and style specific? Which of the well-known indices (e.g., Barra, S&P, Russell or Wilshire) will be selected? Will your international index be in local currency or dollar denominated?

Monitoring Issues

How often do you review the client's portfolio? What does such a review consist of? How do you communicate that with the client? What is the process you use in the monitoring (i.e., what do you monitor for? How often do you do it? How do you get the information for which you are monitoring?)

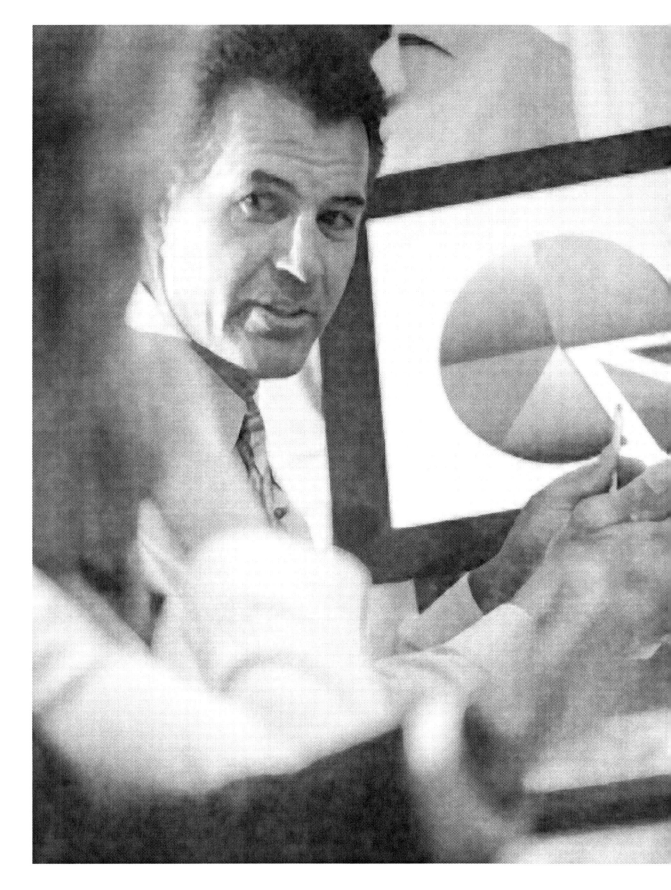

Asset Allocation

A S HAS ALREADY BEEN SUGGESTED, asset allocation is probably the single most important issue to be addressed by an investor and the advisor. As a result, it deserves special attention in the Investment Policy Statement.

If you have not done so already, we strongly encourage you to study Roger C. Gibson's landmark work on this topic *Asset Allocation: Balancing Financial Risk* (3rd edition © 2000, 1996, 1990 published by The McGraw Hill Companies.)

Reflecting the Client's Needs and Risk Tolerance

As we have said earlier and often, we believe that you are not doing your job well if the recommendations you are making to a client do not reflect the client's needs and concerns.

An essential part of the investment process is getting to know your client. That means asking lots of questions *and* listening to the answers. It also means doing the calculations to determine what is necessary to help the client meet stated goals and to learn what is (or is not) possible to achieve.

One of the outcomes of this part of the process should be an identified investment rate that is needed to allow the client to attain their goals. In other words, what is the investment total return that will be necessary for the client to afford the expenses in their current life and those that they want to be able to plan on in their future?

In addition, the advisor should be as clear as possible about the limits of the client's tolerance for risk. It is not going to do you or the client any good if you create a portfolio that periodically declines more than the client is willing to live with. Selling at the market bottom (or on the way down) because they can't stand the volatility hurts the client. The advisor's failure to accurately assess the client's tolerance for risk and to appropriately implement a portfolio that reflects those limits is more often than not the ultimate cause of such panic selling.

As a result, the design of an asset allocation is going to be driven by the level of returns needed by the client, and then limited by the tolerance for declines. Sometimes, the need for return creates a likely volatility that exceeds the client's risk tolerance, or sometimes the required return is unreasonably high. Such a situation leaves few choices, and rarely are they good. Compromises will be needed. If the needed return is so high as to be unachievable, then the advisor needs to help the client adjust the goals. If the needed return can be accomplished, but is still too volatile for the client, then the client has several choices:

- Adjust the goals downward until the required return has a volatility that is acceptable

- Work longer or save more so that the need for returns can be lowered

- Die sooner (generally not an acceptable alternative)

- Learn more about investment history and concepts so their tolerance for volatility/risk increases

Asset allocation is probably the single most important issue to be addressed by an investor and the advisor.

Designing the Portfolio Using an Optimizer

An optimizer is a computer program that helps the portfolio designer (the advisor) find the optimal mix of asset classes (or theoretically, specific assets) given a desired level of risk (thus maximizing probable return) or given a desired investment return (thus minimizing the expected amount of volatility). In essence, the program's purpose is to help you find the most appropriate point on the "efficient frontier curve" that offers the most advantageous risk-reward ratio.

If you are starting with a needed investment return in mind, the optimizer allows you to find that mix of assets that is expected to provide the minimum degree of volatility to which the client's portfolio will be exposed while achieving the hoped-for return. Your purpose is to find an asset allocation that can reasonably be expected to satisfy your client's return needs at the lowest possible risk.

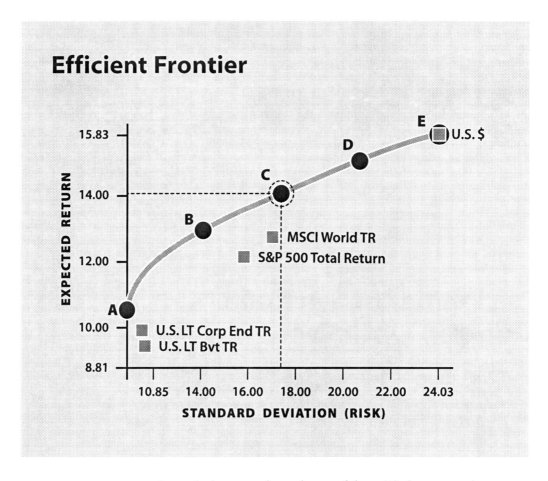

Efficient Frontier

An optimizer uses three classes of data: (1) the expected return for each asset, (2) the expected volatility of each asset, and (3) the expected correlation of movement that each asset has to every other asset in the portfolio. Volatility is measured for this purpose by standard deviation. Correlation is a measure of comparing the movement of one asset to another—if one were to move up by 50 percent, what expectation would exist regarding whether the second asset would move up or down, and by how much?

If you have the mathematical background or tools, you can build your own optimizer program using Excel or some other spreadsheet program. Or there are several commercially available products (for example, from Sungard/Frontier Analytics in San Diego or from Ibbotson Associates in Chicago). These are relatively affordable, are accurately calculated, offer graphics and other features that help explain the output, and they provide the data needed to do the calculations. They are worth the cost.

We do not believe it is responsible investment management to recommend an asset allocation without having a thoughtful, researched process by which such portfolio designs are developed. The most accepted way for this to occur is through the use of a computer-based optimizer. In simple terms, if you are recommending to the client that 30 percent of the client's portfolio consist of large U.S. stocks, you have to be prepared to answer questions like: Why 30 percent? Why not 28 percent or 32 percent? Why are you including each of the asset classes you've chosen, and why have you not included others?

It bears repeating that if the risk/volatility of the portfolio is more than the client is willing to or should bear, then you need to have some more discussions. One option is to have the client make adjustments to their goals (lower the spending, increase the saving, work longer or die sooner) enough so that the needed return would decline to the point where the attendant risk level moves to within an acceptable range.

A second option is to work with the client to educate them more about investment risk and volatility with the hope of raising their inherent tolerance for investment volatility. Don't force the issue! If you set up a portfolio that is inherently riskier than what the client is willing to bear, inevitably you will experience a down market and the client may demand to get out at just the wrong time. The client will be hurt financially and you'll have an unhappy ex-client.

Your purpose is to find an asset allocation that can reasonably be expected to satisfy your client's return needs at the lowest possible risk.

Optimizer Difficulties

While the use of an optimizer is important and very helpful in designing portfolio construction, its "answers" need to be carefully considered and should not be accepted without a critical review. Because of the nature of the optimizer's calculations, it is very sensitive to changes in the data, whether return, volatility or correlation. It often happens that a simple use of the program will lead you to putting an unreasonably large portion of the portfolio into some asset class like leasing programs (because of their purported higher yields and lower volatility), or the program might ignore an asset class like small cap stocks. Effective use of optimizer programs inevitably requires limitations on which asset classes are to be included in the portfolio and the extent to which they will be permitted to employ each such asset class via percentage constraints. Unless you put certain restrictions on the program, optimization will more often than not lead to an unreasonable portfolio design.

Programs like optimizers imply that there is some magical "right answer" to the question of finding the best portfolio design. In fact, there is no one right asset allocation. It would be ideal if each portfolio rested somewhere on the efficient frontier. But the assumptions that go into the calculation drive the result, and these change from advisor to advisor and software manufacturer to software manufacturer. In other words, the efficient frontier and optimal portfolio design are both moving targets, at best. Given that the mathematics involved in optimizer calculations are so sensitive to changes in assumptions used, it is critical that the advisor develop a consistent rationale for how the assumptions are going to be built.

So what are some of the possible differences between two users trying to design a portfolio for two people, given the same risk tolerance level?

- First, they may not agree on which asset classes to include or exclude (for example, should you include emerging markets, mortgages, or foreign bonds?).

- Second, they may not agree on what limits to put on individual asset classes (for example, I don't want more than 30 percent in bonds, or I want to limit emerging markets to no more than 5 percent of the portfolio).

- Third, how do they decide what return assumptions to use—historical data or someone's prediction of future returns? If historical returns are chosen, what period is most representative of what is likely to be experienced in the future? Since 1926? Earlier? The last 30 or 10 years? Is the data equally available for all asset classes? Given that the markets change moment to moment, historical return figures that include the most recent time frame are in constant flux, so whatever assumption you used last month may no longer be the "best" answer.

- Fourth, a similar problem exists for both standard deviation and correlation figures—they change all the time, so which numbers are used?

What the advisor decides about each of these questions affects the answers derived from the calculations. The portfolio you design for your client may differ substantially from what someone else might design working with the same client information.

We think optimization is a good process for the advisor to go through in designing portfolios and asset allocations, but it is critical that the advisor recognize the limitations. Optimization is probably appropriate to help you or your client understand how increasing, decreasing, adding or deleting an asset class might affect the overall risk and return of a portfolio. That can help in making intelligent design choices, but the "answer" that comes out of the computer is not necessarily "right" or even appropriate if

While the use of an optimizer is important and very helpful in designing portfolio construction, its "answers" need to be carefully considered and should not be accepted without a critical review.

Use optimized programs with caution.

unintelligently used or arbitrarily applied. The input provided to the computer software and the context in which it is placed need to be appropriate themselves. The phrase "garbage in, garbage out" truly applies here. Use these programs with caution. Use them as a guide, but don't rely on them for "*the* answer."

Designating Asset Classes

When designing a portfolio, we believe it is important to get agreement first on which asset classes are to be included, and then in what proportion, *before* entering into discussions of what specific security or mutual fund will be used. If you help the client understand the conceptual framework first, then which specific investments (stock, bond or mutual fund) are used is almost an afterthought, requiring very little discussion. If you put your effort into educating the client and helping them understand the rationale for why you are doing things as you are, then you'll find it much easier going when the time comes to identify the specific investments you are recommending they own.

That, of course, begs the question "What asset classes do I use?" Everyone is going to have his or her own take on this decision. For example, at which of the following levels do you prefer to construct a portfolio? Stocks versus bonds, domestic versus foreign, large company versus small company, manager style versus indexed, sectors or diversified—as illustrated below.

- This portfolio will have 70 percent equities

- This portfolio will have 40 percent of the total in U.S. equities

- This portfolio will have 28 percent of the total in large company U.S. equities

- This portfolio will have 15 percent of the total in large company value U.S. equities

- This portfolio will have 2 percent of the total in U.S. auto stocks

Keep in mind that in using the optimizer, you need to have data (return, standard deviation and correlation) that allows it to work for each asset class being chosen. So, one of the limiting factors to your decision may be what level of asset class definition has all the necessary data. Generally, the best choices with this limitation in mind are going to be (1) U.S. equities, (2) large company U.S. equities, or (3) large company value U.S. equities.

One of the problems you can run into when you invest using mutual funds is that oftentimes there is "asset class spillover." In other words, a small cap mutual fund will often carry real estate as part of its holdings, or an international fund will hold companies from emerging market countries, or a U.S. equity fund will hold some non-U.S. companies. Does this mean that you should not create separate asset classes in your portfolio for real estate or emerging markets or international? Does it mean that you decrease the specific allocation, and if you choose this approach, how do you track the changes the manager may make?

The choices we have made in our own companies are (1) to use asset classes at the level of "large U.S. stocks." While we have a bias for value stocks and generally try to weight large stocks 60 percent value and 40 percent growth, we define the class as being large U.S. rather than specify the more refined breakout of growth and value styles. (2) We try to carefully choose the funds we use, for the most part trying to avoid the spillover that limits the flexibility many managers value. Doing so allows us more control. You may have a different answer, but it is critical that you at least recognize and ask the question of yourself.

Reflecting the Asset Allocation in the IPS

As you can see from the example below, we provide both a descriptive matrix and a pie chart to help the client understand how the portfolio design is being constructed.

ASSET ALLOCATION			
CATEGORY	**HOLDINGS**	**PERCENT**	**TOTAL**
Cash			**1%**
	Money Market Funds	1%	
Bonds			**39%**
	Municipal Bonds	23%	
	Corp/Gov't Bonds	16%	
	Foreign Bonds		
	High Yield Bonds		
Equities			**55%**
	U.S. Large Stocks	25%	
	U.S. Small Socks	11%	
	International Stocks	15%	
	Emerging Mkt Stocks	4%	
Real Estate			**5%**
	REITs	5%	
	Direct Ownership		
Alternative Investments			
	Hedge Funds		
	Commodity Funds		
TOTAL		**100%**	**100%**

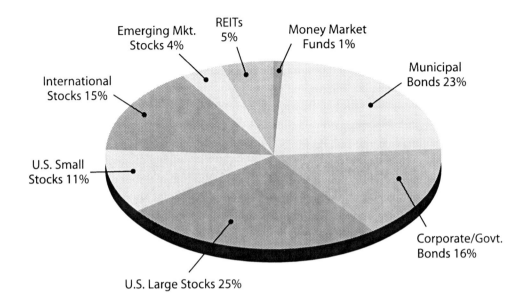

International Stocks 15%

Emerging Mkt. Stocks 4%

REITs 5%

Money Market Funds 1%

Municipal Bonds 23%

U.S. Small Stocks 11%

Corporate/Govt. Bonds 16%

U.S. Large Stocks 25%

Addressing Expected Returns

Assuming that the construction of the portfolio has been done with the end results in mind, then the IPS should identify what those end results are. In the section on Investment Objectives, the IPS addresses what the client wants from the portfolio. In the Asset Allocation section, it is appropriate to identify what is reasonable to expect from the portfolio as constructed. This is your justification for having designed the portfolio as you have.

The questions to address in this section of the IPS are:

1. What return can the client expect in the future, given how the portfolio has been designed?

2. What range of returns is possible for the client to experience (and ideally identify a statistical probability, such as, "at a 95 percent confidence level")?

3. How might this change over different time periods?

It is appropriate to identify what is reasonable to expect from the portfolio as constructed. This is your justification for having designed the portfolio as you have.

To get the answers to this level of detail requires optimizer software. If you don't use an optimizer or the portfolio designer does not provide these answers, then realistically the advisor should not attempt to include them in the IPS.

Here's an example of how portfolio returns can be portrayed in an IPS:

Historical Portfolio Returns & Volatility

The Investor's willingness to accept risk and their expectation for investment growth have a direct bearing on the rate of return objective for this portfolio.

The following historical returns reflect the results of this portfolio, as constructed, from 1972 to 2001 (30 years) had this same portfolio existed over that period.

Bear in mind, these outcomes represent historical results using index data and estimated expenses. It should be recognized that the portfolio will invest in mutual funds or other securities and that the actual weighting of these securities can and will vary. It is also important to note that the future returns of the securities in the portfolio can be expected to vary from the historical returns referenced.

The portfolio results referenced reflect a portfolio design having a "value" orientation (that is, employing funds or stocks with below-average price-to-book ratios). Historically, over-weighting "value" investments in a portfolio has resulted in higher portfolio returns with lower risk when compared with portfolios with greater "growth" characteristics. The Investor's portfolio will be designed with a "value" orientation.

The portfolio's historical rate of return is not a guarantee of future investment returns. Future returns could differ significantly and capital loss is possible. This Investment Policy Statement shall not be construed as offering a guarantee.

Historical Rolling Period Real Returns (1972 to 2001)	ROLLING 1 YEAR PERIODS	ROLLING 5 YEAR PERIODS
Annualized Returns:		
Best Period	38.7%	19.2%
Average (arithmetic mean)	4.9%	5.7%
Worst Period	−32.1%	−4.1%
% of Periods Generating:		
Negative returns	29.2%	12.6%
Less than CPI + 4%	49.9%	35.5%
Portfolio Return (geometric mean)	11.4%	10.0%
Minus Estimated Expenses	1.7%	
Portfolio Return (net)	9.7%	
Minus Inflation (5.0% + 0.3% compounding)	5.3%	1.2%
Real Return After Inflation	4.4%	

The returns reflected above are *after* inflation and include price appreciation, dividends, and interest, and are net of 1.7 percent estimated mutual fund management expenses and advisory fees. They assume use of taxable bonds (municipal bonds yield less but are assumed to return about the same after taxes). Calculations do not include the impact of transaction costs or income taxes.

Managing expectations is one of the more critical things we do for clients.

There are several things to note about the above description of returns:

- Annualized returns are provided for both the one-year and five-year periods to show how good and bad years tend to offset one another, thus moderating a portfolio's volatility over time.

- The returns displayed are real returns; in other words, inflation has been subtracted to show what is left to increase the value of the portfolio.

- The returns displayed are after estimated fees and expenses. These are *net real returns* to the investor.

- The display shows the best and worst 12-month period and 60-month periods over the last 30 years. It does not just rely on calendar year data, but on rolling periods (for example, from August 1 to the following July 31). This approach offers the client a real world example of how bad it could get, even for a relatively conservative portfolio.

- Also identified are the proportion of 12- and 60-month periods that were negative in results, or the frequency with which this portfolio would not have achieved the investment objective of inflation plus 4 percent, net of fees.

- The underlying assumptions about returns (geometric returns, expenses assumed, inflation rate used) so they can be clearly discussed with and understood by the client.

These calculations were done using the software program "Analyst" from Ibbotson Associates and data from Ibbotson and Dimensional Fund Advisors.

Managing expectations is one of the more critical things we do for clients. Having this data and being able to discuss it with clients is an important element of serving them well. It gives them a realistic and comprehensive understanding of the real world. Future declines are unlikely to surprise them and therefore they are unlikely to panic-sell at the worst times.

So, what if you don't have the use of an optimizer?

Without an optimizer, it is unclear to us how you would be able to identify the possible range of future returns. More importantly, if you can't identify the possible range of future returns, how can you be confident that the portfolio you have designed for your client satisfies their risk tolerance limitations, that expected results don't exceed the declines they are willing to accept?

Obviously, if you can't identify the possible range of returns, you can't make any predictions about how the long-term volatility will decrease over time.

If you can't identify the possible range of returns, you can't make any predictions about how the long-term volatility will decrease over time.

A Second Approach

Remembering that the objective in your asset allocation discussions is to manage your client's expectations by providing them with some insights regarding what might occur (especially on the downside) with their portfolio, it is not necessary to be as complete as the prior section implies. Here's another way to provide some insight:

	ONE YEAR	TEN YEAR
Maximum for Period	28.2%	16.4%
Estimated Average	8.9%	8.9%
Minimum for Period	−12.3%	2.6%
"Worst Case Conditions"	−21.3%	-0.5%

All return calculations herein include price appreciation/depreciation, income distributions and capital gains distributions. Above figures based on 95 percent statistical likelihood, except for those of "Worst Case Conditions,"

There is no absolute rule that says you must include expected returns and variability in your Investment Policy Statements.

which returns are expected to exceed all but 5 percent of the time. Calculations do not include the impact of management fees, transaction costs or taxes.

On average, over long periods of time, this portfolio design can be expected to experience losses two in eight years, and in such cases should take an average of somewhat less than ten months to recover such losses. Over a five-year period, such a portfolio's performance should exceed inflation 72 percent of the time.

Again, the information about returns, about the variability of expected returns, and about how often the returns should beat inflation comes from optimizer software or from the provider of your portfolio design.

A Simpler Approach

The detail and the information described above may be beyond what you are currently able to do in your office. Assuming that you have no resources available to help you with this (head office, research department, investment strategy group, your broker/dealer), then you need to consider how you can help your client understand what is reasonable to expect. We've listed at the end of this chapter some available resources for your consideration.

There is no absolute rule that says you must include expected returns and variability in your Investment Policy Statements. We think it is a good practice and doing so will separate you from your competition, but it is not critical that you do it.

It is possible to come pretty close to identifying a portfolio's expected return by simply calculating a weighted average. For example, if you are going to put two-thirds of the portfolio in stocks (assume 9 percent returns) and one-third in bonds (assume

6 percent returns), then by multiplying two-thirds times 9 percent and one-third times 6 percent and then adding the two answers together, you would reasonably be able to say that such a portfolio has an expected return of 8 percent. That expected return is pretty close to what an optimizer program would calculate. Then you should decide whether to subtract out the investment or advisor expenses to produce a net investment return to the client. We recommend that you do.

To gather data on past returns for the asset classes you will be using, we suggest the use of index-based calculations; but it is also possible to use broad-based mutual funds, like the Vanguard S&P 500 or their Total Market Index. Morningstar's software also offers plenty of information about portfolios built of investments on which they report.

While we don't endorse or encourage you to present your recommendations in the following way, we are realistic enough to recognize that not everyone is going to go to the trouble and expense of buying optimizer software, learning how to use it, collecting appropriate data and then running the program for each client. Therefore, we offer the following as an alternative way to present your client with a picture of what might happen to their portfolio:

> The portfolio proposed in this Investment Policy Statement can reasonably be expected to provide the investor with an annual return of 8.9 percent, calculated using a weighted average of the historical returns of each asset class in their respective proportions. The actual returns will vary from this number, sometimes quite broadly, both up and down. Over time, good years and bad years have had a tendency to balance out one another, so that despite the inevitable volatility of this portfolio, as the results average out they will begin to approach the above-stated expected annual investment return.

A basic decision is whether to use history as a guide or try to create expected future returns.

Identifying Your Assumptions

One of the basic decisions each advisor needs to make is whether you want to help the client understand what to expect from their portfolio by (1) making predictions about what is likely to happen in the future or (2) simply to report what would have happened to such a portfolio in the past. The latter relies on historical data (and history may or may not be similar to what will happen in the future), while the former relies on an attempt by the advisor (or someone) to estimate what will happen in the future. One is factual, but possibly of little relevance, while the other is pure speculation. Our position on this question is that relying on factual history will serve you better. As a result, we do not speak of "expected returns" but only of what would have happened to this kind of portfolio in the past. Hence, the title of the section that provides data assumptions is "Historical Portfolio and Asset Class Returns." Had we taken the other choice, the section would be titled "Expected Portfolio and Asset Class Returns."

Whichever way you decide to go on this question, you need to provide a record of the data you were using at the time to reach the conclusions you did. To be able to calculate a portfolio's expected or historical return, you needed to use information about the assets making up that portfolio. We think it is important to share that information with your client.

Think of it this way—if sometime in the future you are questioned about why you chose to recommend a particular portfolio, you will want to have a record of the inputs you used when you are deciding on a particular asset allocation design. All that is necessary for this section of the IPS is to record that information. For example:

Historical Portfolio & Asset Class Returns (1972 to 2001)		
ASSET CLASS	**HISTORICAL RETURN**	**STANDARD DEVIATION**
Asset Class Returns (before expenses):		
Cash	6.6%	0.8%
Intermediate Bonds	8.5%	4.9%
U.S. Large Stocks	12.2%	17.5%
U.S. Small Stocks	13.3%	24.8%
International Stocks	11.2%	19.1%
Emerging Market Stocks*	11.3%	27.8%
Real Estate	12.5%	15.4%

* Emerging Market data since 1988

Resources

If you are not currently employing some of the "best practices" described in this chapter, we recommend that you contact one or more of the resources in this section to gain the ability to intelligently discuss and perform portfolio optimization for your clients or to simply have the ability to make an intelligent guess about what behavior and performance your client is likely to experience.

Ibbotson Associates

(www.Ibbotson.com) (800) 758-3557

"Ibbotson Associates has been providing the investment industry with revolutionary software and data for more than a decade. Today, the firm continues to utilize cutting-edge technology to provide end-users with easy-to-use, graphical software. Our unique approach has earned Ibbotson Associates the reputation as a leading provider of innovative investment tools in the financial industry." Ibbotson's "Investment Planning Software and Data addresses tax rates, client information and individual risk tolerances—the top concerns of client-minded financial planners and brokers."

Frontier Analytics

(www.online.sungard.com/frontier/) (858) 552-1268

"Frontier is a professional asset allocation platform that provides reliable advice and analytics to brokerage firms, banks, insurance companies, accounting firms, and independent investment advisors. Frontier's Web-enabled calculation engines and historical performance data provide advanced portfolio optimization, financial projection, risk profiling and implementation planning tools, as well as generate investment policy statements and handle tax and cash flows. Recognized for their ease of use and high quality graphs and reports, Frontier technology is considered the industry standard for asset allocation. AllocationMaster™ and FactMaster™ are investment analysis applications designed to meet the needs of investment advisors working with individual investors. Investment Plus™ and Simulation Plus™ provide analytical tools for institutional investors."

AdvisoryWorld

(formerly Wilson Associates)
(www.advisoryworld.com) (800) 480-3888

"AdvisoryWorld brings investment professionals and personal investors together with the most comprehensive and easy-to-use interactive financial and advisory tools and services. These integrated financial tools include Internet based multi-asset portfolio modeling, a revolutionary way of finding optimal financial solutions by integrating optimization and Monte Carlo simulation, financial plan analysis, detailed cash flow, security analysis and, later this year, portfolio management and performance reporting. These Internet based products are available in professional and personal investor models." AdvisoryWorld also appears to be testing a Web-based product that might prove attractive for advisors not ready to purchase their own software. Depending on the product, pricing is from less than $30 a month to just under $1,000.

Morningstar

(www.morningstar.com or http://advisor.morningstar.com)
(312) 696-6000

Morningstar is best known for its analysis of mutual funds and their star-rating system. The Principia Pro software and the new Web-bonded "Advisor Work Station" offer quite a bit of data as well as some helpful portfolio analysis. They both allow the user to back-test how a proposed portfolio would have performed.

Portfolio Selection Systems

(www.portfolionetworks.com/main.html) (352) 377-4525

"PSS publishes a state of the art portfolio selection software package PSS Release 2.0: Digital Portfolio Theory. PSS gives the investor the ability to efficiently achieve market timing and optimal diversification by applying digital signal processing to the classical Modern Portfolio Theory portfolio selection problem."

PerTrac 2000

(www.pertrac2000.com/allocation.asp) (901) 888-7500

"One of the most useful analytical functions within PerTrac 2000 is the ability to create composite portfolios and composite benchmarks. Whether you are building a portfolio of mutual funds, hedge funds, separately managed accounts, funds-of-funds, or in-house investments, you will find the allocation tools within PerTrac 2000 to be both powerful and intuitive. Currently, the following databases are PerTrac 2000 compatible: Nelson, Morningstar, Hedge Fund Research (HFR), International Traders Research (ITR), Stark, MAR, Hedgefund.net, Mobius, PIPER, Altvest, and Tass. Also, two free index databases are included with PerTrac 2000 that combine for a total of approximately 1,600 benchmarks." The single user version starts at $5,000.

Fidelity Investments

(www.Fidelity.com)

Fidelity offers its investors a "Planning Center" in which they offer some decent tools for portfolio analysis:

Analyze Your Current Portfolio
A service for Fidelity customers, Fidelity portfolio analysis provides expanded information about your portfolio (or a portion of your portfolio) by:

- "Giving both graphical and holdings views of your account assets

- Showing your asset allocation, foreign and domestic stock exposure, and industry weightings

- Comparing the industry sector weightings of your selected equity portfolio against the Wilshire 5000® Total Market Index

- Mapping your equity holdings style

- Detailing some historical information about how your current asset mix has performed over certain periods of time"

Dimensional Fund Advisors

(www.dfafunds.com)

DFA is known for its academic-based investment approach. As a result, it primarily offers passive index funds. But it is also a great source for data. It offers "CRSP: Dimensional's Data Source, The

Center for Research in Securities Prices." DFA tends to be selective about the advisors it works with, but for those using DFA, they can be very helpful.

Solver.com

(www.solver.com) (888) 831-0333

"The Premium Solver Platform includes a Quadratic Solver extension to its Simplex-based Solver for linear programming problems. This LP/Quadratic Solver easily handles "efficient portfolio" models…, using the Markowitz or Sharpe methods—it is faster and more accurate for these problems than the standard Excel Solver. The Premium Solver Platform is highly recommended if you are solving portfolio optimization problems." Using an Excel add-in that costs a few hundred dollars, you can get help with:

● "Theory—Display this worksheet for a brief discussion of the theory of efficient portfolios and the principles of duration matching in bond portfolios

● Markowitz—Portfolio Optimization—Markowitz Model: Allocate funds to stocks to minimize risk for a target rate of return—assumes that variances and covariances are known

● Full Markowitz—Portfolio Optimization—Markowitz Model: Allocate funds to stocks to minimize risk for a target rate of return—calculates variances and covariances from historical stock prices

● Efficient Frontier—Stock Portfolio Management: Uses a VBA program to optimize several scenarios for minimum risk at different target rates of return, then draws a graph of the efficient frontier

● Sharpe—Portfolio Optimization—Sharpe Model (CAPM): Uses Excel's regression functions to calculate alphas and betas for stocks relative to a market index, then uses these to find an efficient portfolio"

Building an Investment Policy Statement

The Components of an IPS

EACH INVESTMENT POLICY STATEMENT should be unique, reflecting the specific situation of the investor. Depending upon the type of investor, the format of the statement will differ. In Appendix B, there are different templates to address the varying requirements of:

- An individual/married investor

- A family trust

- A charitable remainder trust

You can modify the templates for your own needs.

- An endowment or a foundation

- A pension plan

- A profit-sharing plan

- A 401(k) plan

- A variable life insurance policy held in a trust

These Investment Policy Statement template documents should not be used as a substitute for a tailored Investment Policy Statement that is specifically developed for the needs and circumstances of each plan or client.

Understanding the need to adapt the Investment Policy Statement to the unique requirements of each investor, there are, however, some common components of each Investment Policy Statement.

An Investment Policy Statement has six common components:

1. Key factual and account information and summary of investor circumstances

2. Investment objectives, time horizon and risk attitudes

3. Permissible asset classes, constraints and restrictions

4. The asset allocation

5. Selection, monitoring and control procedures

6. Signatures

1. Account Information and Summary of Investor Circumstances

The IPS should include key quantitative and qualitative factors about the investor or the investing entity, such as:

- Background and purpose for the money

- Approximate amount of assets subject to the Investment Policy Statement

- Authorized decision makers

- Names or positions of each trustee, if appropriate

- Custodian for the investment accounts, account numbers and tax ID numbers

- Names, addresses and phone numbers of the investment advisor, custodian, plan administrator, accountant and attorney

- Fiduciary bonding (carrier, contract number, amount), where appropriate

- Investor's key economic assumptions regarding the investor's future

- The current investment environment and the overall outlook for the broader economy

For individual investors and trusts, you should also include:

- The current marginal tax rate and other relevant facts about their tax status

- Ages, health and general financial status of investor or beneficiary

- Summary of current income and expenses of investor

- Outlook for the future for their personal financial circumstances

Each Investment Policy Statement should be unique, specifically developed for the needs and circumstances of the investor.

For endowments and foundations, you should also include:

- Distribution philosophy or spending policy
- Anticipated funding and distribution amounts, timing and, to the extent possible, a five-year projection

For retirement plans you should also include:

- Number of employees covered
- Vesting schedule and current asset values
- Date of plan adoption and last amendment
- Plan year-end
- Timing of anticipation of plan distribution
- Anticipated funding and distribution amounts annually for the next five years
- Intent to comply with Section 404(c) requirements (401(k) plans only)

For variable life policies in an insurance trust, you should also include:

- All the vital information on the insurance contract
- Information about the investment choices and management
- Information about the trust and the trustee(s)

2. Identification, Discussion, and Review of Investment Objectives, Time Horizon, and Attitude About and Tolerance for Risk

Investing is best done with a purpose in mind.

It is important that in this section the Investment Policy Statement records the following:

- The investor's investment goals

- The investor's target rate of return

- The time horizon over which this return is expected

- Attitudes about risk, including the maximum amount of decline in portfolio values the investor will accept as a tolerable "worst case" one-year scenario

- Some discussion about the investor's financial capacity to take on risk, and any limitations it may impose

Time horizon, risk and return are related. As we have previously discussed, to determine an appropriate target rate of return, an investor must simultaneously address their tolerance for portfolio volatility (risk) and their desired rate of return within the context of their investment time horizon.

Goals

Investing is best done with a purpose in mind. Discussion of the investor's goals may generally include any or some of the following:

- Preserving the purchasing power of principal by maintaining a real rate of return (after taxes, if applicable) at a certain level above inflation

- Growth of capital

- Meeting required liquidity, purchase or income objectives

The target rate of return an investor wants to achieve should be stated in relation to a given benchmark.

- Minimizing current income taxes

- Keeping year-to-year negative fluctuations of portfolio values below a stated amount (such as 10 percent)

If the investor has any other specific or general goals for the investments, they should be identified in this section.

Target Rate of Return

The target rate of return an investor wants to achieve should be stated in relation to a given benchmark, such as inflation, the S&P 500 or a customized benchmark of asset classes. We believe it is inappropriate to use a fixed rate of return, such as 10 percent. For example, if the desired rate of return is 8 percent when inflation is 3 percent, the target real rate of return is 5 percent (8% − 3% = 5%). When inflation is 6 percent, a client is unlikely to be as pleased with an 8 percent return. In the long run, a relative rate of return is more realistic in the context of a client attaining their goals.

The investor needs to understand historical returns for different asset categories. By understanding the historical relationships and risk/reward trade-offs between various asset classes, clients can internalize important concepts, such as the difference between short-term volatility and long-term return possibilities. For example, on average, stock returns have exceeded inflation by 6 percent to 8 percent a year, according to Ibbotson Associates. Bond returns have exceeded inflation by only 1 percent to 3 percent and cash has tended to barely beat inflation at all over time. Even if these returns are not exactly duplicated, the historical relationships revealed by these relative returns are likely to hold among asset classes going forward over the long term. Clients should understand that it is imprudent to expect different risk/return profiles (for example, cash outperforming stocks over any length of time).

Time Horizon

"Time horizon" is the time over which you want to achieve a specific goal. For example, an individual investor who has a goal of maintaining their standard of living for the balance of their life would have a time horizon equal to their life expectancy.

It is critical to establish how long the assets to be invested are likely to stay invested. In other words, how long before partial or full liquidation is likely? And when it occurs, to what extent is it likely to occur?

Time horizon is important for determining which types of assets are appropriate for use in a portfolio. The shorter the time horizon, the less volatility can be tolerated. For that reason, stocks or long-term bonds would be a poor choice for investors who need to sell their investments within a relatively short time. We believe that stocks and long-term bonds are poor investment choices (due to their short-term volatility) if the time horizon for that asset is less than five years. For example, ERISA plans or trusts that have the potential to require cash disbursements may not be good candidates for having all their assets invested in volatile investments, such as stocks or long-term bonds.

If the investment time frame is long, temporary declines are to be expected and generally can be better tolerated. The pain of accepting short-term declines must be accepted in exchange for the chance to achieve the reward of higher long-term gains. Riskier investments fluctuate more in value than do so-called "safe" investments. The broader the range of possible outcomes the investor is willing to tolerate over the short term, the higher the long-term rate of return that investor can target.

Attitudes About and Tolerance for Risk or Volatility

In the past, risk was considered something to be avoided. Now, acceptance of risk must be incorporated in the investment policy. The standard for measuring risk has shifted from an asset-by-asset basis to an overall portfolio basis.

Assets that may, by themselves, be considered risky may actually lower risk when combined in appropriate proportions with

Time horizon is important for determining which types of assets are appropriate for use in a portfolio. The shorter the time horizon, the less volatility can be tolerated.

The broader the range of possible outcomes the investor is willing to tolerate over the short term, the higher the long-term rate of return that investor can target.

other asset classes. For example, managed futures would not be considered prudent as an investment if the whole portfolio were made up of such investments. But things change if managed futures make up a small portion (2–3 percent) of a portfolio that also includes foreign and domestic stocks, bonds, real estate, and cash. Many studies have suggested that including managed futures actually lowers the risk of the total portfolio due to its lack of or lower correlation with the other asset classes. In other words, despite what otherwise might appear to be excessive risk, holding managed futures can actually moderate the swings in total portfolio value because managed futures tend to move in the opposite direction, in many circumstances, relative to the major asset classes.

Therefore, modern investment theory argues that it is necessary to look at the risk of the total portfolio to determine an acceptable level and that considering each asset class in isolation probably leads to inappropriate conclusions.

There are a variety of investment risks, each of which has been addressed in places throughout this Investment Policy Statement model. The kind of risk most investors are concerned with is the loss of principal value. That issue should be addressed in this section.

History suggests that the more downside volatility an investor is willing to accept, the greater the potential return. If an investor is unwilling to accept any drop in the value of the portfolio for any period of time, then the best returns that could be hoped for will usually approximate inflation over the long term. Since most investors will want to attain returns above inflation, they must be willing to tolerate occasional drops in value.

This section of the IPS establishes a range of downside returns that will be accepted by the investor in exchange for the possibility of achieving returns above the inflation rate. By quantifying this acceptable range for the portfolio as a whole, the trustees or fiduciaries go on record as stating that declines are acceptable and to be expected.

There cannot be any guarantees about portfolio performance, up or down. Therefore, when these lower limits are established, the statistical likelihood of the specified limits being exceeded should be identified.

Establishing downside limits and statistical probabilities might be worded similarly to the following:

> The Investor is willing to accept a portfolio designed to fluctuate between +28 percent and −10 percent annually (with a 95 percent probability and with a mean expected return of 9 percent). Separate parts of the portfolio may fluctuate more than the total portfolio.

The Financial Capacity to Accept Risk

Individual clients may be willing to accept risk, but it might also be that given their financial circumstances, it would be imprudent for them to do so. Thus, the Investment Policy Statement needs to address the financial circumstances of the client, to the extent the circumstances will limit the client's ability to withstand risk. Any of the following could limit an investor's financial capacity to take on risk and therefore all should be addressed:

- Adequacy of insurance coverages
- Number of dependents and the extent of their dependency
- Other available financial resources
- Size, stability and frequency of income
- Debt obligations

3. Permitted Assets, Constraints and Restrictions

This third section adds the final information and data-building blocks so that in the next section, the actual asset allocation can be determined. Topics to be discussed in Section 3 include:

- The asset classes selected for investment

- The asset classes restricted from investment

- The liquidity and marketability requirements

- The maximum and minimum parameters, if any, for each asset class within the portfolio

- Limits on the concentration of investments in the portfolio

- The purchase or liquidation strategy

Selected Asset Classes

A number of asset categories are available for any investment portfolio. Only the rare portfolio will contain all categories. The major categories are:

1. **Cash and cash equivalents**
    (money market funds, Treasury bills, etc.)

2. **Fixed-income investments**
    (bonds and interest-bearing instruments)
    - Foreign
    - Domestic
    - Further segmented by credit quality or investment grade, issuer, tax status, maturity, duration and geography

3. **Stocks**
    - Foreign
    - Domestic
    - Further segmented by market capitalization, investment style, geography or sectors

4. **Real estate**
    - Direct ownership
    - Indirect ownership by securities or limited partnership
    - Further segmented by type, geography and marketability

5. **Tangible assets**
   - Precious metals
   - Natural resources

6. **Alternative investment assets**
   - Business/venture capital investments
   - Hedge funds
   - Option strategies
   - Community futures
   - Merger/arbitrage opportunities
   - Noncorrelated assets (such as timber)

Restricted Asset Classes

For a variety of reasons, an investor may choose to avoid one or more of these major asset classes or a subset of any of them. If so, these should be identified to create a record of such desires and to preclude them from being used within the investment portfolio.

Securities Guidelines

In those cases in which individual securities are to be used instead of funds, it would be desirable to provide the money managers with guidelines about what kinds of securities or securities transactions are not to be included in the portfolio. For example:

1. Restricted or unregistered stocks, commodities or commodity contracts, short sales, or purchases on margin.

2. Pledging, hypothecating, or lending securities.

3. Investments in companies not meeting certain standards, such as length of time in operation, nonprofitable companies, or investments that exceed some percentage of total company ownership.

   It may also be desirable to provide specific guidelines about permissible securities within each asset class.

Also, should the investor or advisor have a bias toward using index-type investments, the details of this preference should be noted in this section.

Other

The Investment Policy Statement might also discuss any other issues important to the investor, such as the investor's view toward derivative investments (say, futures and options), short selling, margin transactions or the purchase of insurance contracts.

Liquidity

Generally, liquidity measures the ability to readily convert an asset to cash, independent of any changes in the economy, without risk of principal loss. For these purposes, we are defining liquidity as the amount of cash or cash equivalents in the portfolio.

Liquidity is needed for a variety of reasons. For example, in a company retirement plan, liquidity is generally needed to pay benefits to terminating employees. In a personal trust, liquidity may be needed to make payments to the beneficiaries of the trust. The Investment Policy Statement should identify how much liquidity the investor requires. Minimum amounts (in dollars or portfolio percentage) should be clarified.

The appropriate level of liquidity may differ from time to time, so periodic review is needed. Such a review should be based upon a projection of possible future cash requirements and their likelihood.

Marketability

Marketability is the relative ability to turn assets into cash and the rapidity with which it can be done (although it may be subject to some loss of principal).

Unanticipated events will inevitably occur. As a result, it is always possible that the projected requirement for liquidity could at one time or another be too low. To meet those unexpected demands on cash, it is possible that it would be necessary to sell assets. The more marketable such assets, the more readily they can be turned into cash.

Most publicly held stocks, bonds and mutual funds can be sold (although sometimes at a loss if the sale occurs at an inopportune time) and turned into cash in a few days. Real estate, private mortgages, venture capital investments, partnerships and certain other types of investments cannot be readily converted to cash. The larger the percentage of nonmarketable investments in a portfolio, the more marketability risk is inherent in that portfolio.

On the other hand, rarely do investors need to turn their entire portfolio into cash at one time. In fact, if we accept the normal assumption that a premium return is awarded in the marketplace for illiquidity, then investors may be disadvantaged if 100 percent of their portfolio is composed of fully marketable securities. Therefore, it may be preferable to put some percentage into nonmarketable investments. How much nonmarketable investments is appropriate is the question.

The larger the percentage of nonmarketable investments in a portfolio, the more marketability risk is inherent in that portfolio.

Flexible Asset Class Targets

Some investors believe in a flexible approach to setting target percentages for asset classes within a portfolio to allow for tactical shifts. In such cases, each asset class will be assigned a currently appropriate target percentage, and a permanent range within which all future targets must reside. For such investors, the Investment Policy Statement should specify the maximum and minimum permitted limits, as well as the current target. For example, we may initially choose to have stocks comprise 45 percent of our portfolio, but in no case are we willing to permit that portion to fall below 30 percent of the portfolio, nor may it ever exceed 65 percent.

Investment Concentration

To restrict the portfolio from "putting too many eggs in one basket," any limitations imposed on the amount of investment must be specified, such as for:

- A single security
- Geographic region
- Industry
- Bond maturity/duration range

Two examples of a limitation might be:

> No single asset (an individual stock, bond, partnership, or mutual fund) shall be permitted to represent more than 10 percent of the aggregate assets of the portfolio unless specifically authorized by the investor in writing.
>
> At all times there must be a minimum of six investments or mutual funds or investment managers represented among the portfolio assets. There shall be no maximum limit to the number of investments, assuming the investor is not disadvantaged by portfolio expenses.

Purchase/Sale Strategy

If the investor has an emotional issue regarding a specific security, such as one inherited from a loved one or especially low-basis stock, and the investor does not want it sold under any circumstances, this fact should be identified in this section.

If the policy prescribes certain procedures to be followed (for example, all new money will be invested using a dollar-cost averaging method over the subsequent 12 months), then those procedures should be detailed as part of the investment policy.

If assets are occasionally being transferred from one custodian to another, is there a consistent policy regarding who will make the sale of the security to be disposed of if new securities are to be purchased? If so, such a policy should be described.

4. The Allocation of Portfolio Assets

In this section the Investment Policy Statement should record the following:

- The asset allocation model to be employed for the portfolio

- The statistical assumptions used to develop the model

- The likely performance and possible range of returns that either would have been produced by the portfolio in the past or can be expected for the portfolio in the future, based upon its design

- The method to be used for portfolio rebalancing

As we have discussed previously, academic research suggests that asset allocation decisions within a portfolio of various asset classes is far more significant in determining portfolio performance than the selection of individual securities, the timing of purchases or sales, and random luck. This research, coupled with the investment strategies of modem portfolio theory, derived from the work of 1990 Nobel laureates Harry Markowitz and William Sharpe, provides the justification for the concept and use of asset allocation.

Further, it is incumbent upon the financial advisor to assist the investor in considering all reasonable asset classes and the different proportions in which they can be combined. Not doing so invites the suggestion of imprudence.

Any number of computer-based programs is available to professional advisors to help them optimize their clients' portfolios. Their educated and reasoned use by the advisor is strongly recommended. Furthermore, if the design of an investment portfolio is subject to litigation, an effective defense has been the proper use of cutting-edge investment technology made possible by such optimization programs.

It is incumbent upon the financial advisor to assist the investor in considering all reasonable asset classes and the different proportions in which they can be combined.

(Note: As previously discussed, the results of any calculation program, including optimizers, are solely dependent upon the inputs, constraints and assumptions available to that program. Prudent use of optimization software requires an understanding and regular review of these considerations to ensure their continued appropriateness.)

Asset Allocation Assumptions

Each time asset classes are allocated to form a portfolio, certain assumptions are made. These should be listed. For example, what assumptions are being made about the annual returns that may occur for each of the asset classes? What level of risk (standard deviation) is expected? What asset class correlation factors are being used?

Sample Allocation for John Doe

(Age 45, with a net worth of $3 million)
Note: The following is an example only. Each investor will require a unique model.

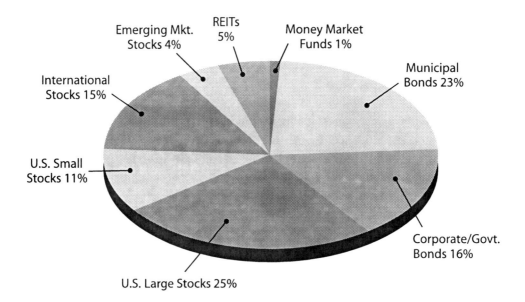

ASSET ALLOCATION			
CATEGORY	**HOLDINGS**	**PERCENT**	**TOTAL**
Cash			**1%**
	Money Market Funds	1%	
Bonds			**39%**
	Municipal Bonds	23%	
	Corp/Gov't Bonds	16%	
	Foreign Bonds		
	High Yield Bonds		
Equities			**55%**
	U.S. Large Stocks	25%	
	U.S. Small Socks	11%	
	International Stocks	15%	
	Emerging Mkt Stocks	4%	
Real Estate			**5%**
	REITs	5%	
	Direct Ownership		
Alternative Investments			
	Hedge Funds		
	Commodity Funds		
TOTAL		**100%**	**100%**

Diversification within Asset Classes

In addition to diversifying among different asset classes according to the asset allocation model, it is imperative that further diversification within each class be considered. Specifically for:

1. **Fixed Income Securities**

   a) Diversify among maturities

   b) Diversify among quality

   c) Diversify among identity of issuers

2. **Real Estate**

   a) Diversify geographically

   b) Diversify among property types

   c) Consider diversifying among property managers

3. **Stocks**

   a) Diversify among issuers

   b) Diversify among industries

   c) Diversify among geographic economies

4. **Mutual Funds or Investment Managers**

   a) Diversify among management styles

   b) Diversify among specialties or focus

Rebalancing

While there are many rebalancing approaches—including market timing and tactical asset allocation—strategic asset allocation tends to be most consistent with long-term focused Investment Policy Statements. Strategic asset allocation works in conjunction with the target percentages described above. The Investment Policy Statement will determine the upper and lower bounds of the target allocation and then state that rebalancing will occur when the upper and lower bounds are exceeded. For example, the investment committee may choose to rebalance whenever any category is more than 10 percent above or below its target range. Should a target of 60 percent be established for equities, then any time the allocation to equities exceeds 70 percent or falls below 50 percent, the portfolio should be rebalanced.

As we have identified in the "Asset Allocation" chapter, the question of when rebalancing is called for should also be addressed. By clearly identifying the rebalancing strategy to be used, or philosophy to be followed, a systematic, disciplined approach is ensured. Using some kind of rebalancing approach has the additional benefit of compelling the investor to sell assets when prices are high and to buy assets when prices are low—a good practice that in the long run is a proven formula for investment success. For further discussion, see the section on rebalancing above under "Difficult Policy Issues."

5. Selecting and Monitoring Advisors/Management and Control Procedures

This section addresses four separate, but related, issues having to do with using outside investment managers and advisors:

- How to select them
- Duties and responsibilities of managers
- How to monitor their performance and their adherence to the investment policy
- How to implement control procedures

Manager Selection

As a general rule, we believe it is advantageous to use multiple managers. While this makes it more complex to select and monitor the managers, it permits the selection of different experts in each

Performance cannot adequately be viewed except in context with risk levels.

major asset class, as well as offering the opportunity to utilize managers following divergent strategies.

The criteria for selecting investment managers should be spelled out to introduce more objectivity into the process. A fact sheet with information about each manager can facilitate the decision-making by the investor or trustee, enabling the process to be more disciplined, objective and factual.

Some of the important areas to be considered include the following:

1. **Performance relative to peers.** Each manager should be identified by their investment objective and investment style in order to compare apples to apples. Viewing the performance of a small capitalization value style manager against that of a large capitalization growth style manager is misleading.

2. **Performance relative to an appropriate benchmark.** When reviewing manager performance, it is important to use a fair standard of comparison. Because different asset classes react differently to economic circumstances, to judge one asset class by an index consisting of another asset class is likely to be misleading. For example, using the large-cap oriented Standard & Poor's 500 Index is inappropriate in conjunction with a small stock fund.

3. **Performance in both rising and falling markets.** How well does the manager react defensively in falling markets and take advantage of rising markets? To ensure a complete picture of both upside and downside risks and returns, it is generally desirable to give the manager an opportunity to perform over a full market cycle.

4. **Risk-adjusted performance.** Performance cannot adequately be viewed except in context with risk levels. Investment with higher risk levels must achieve better than normal returns to compensate the investor for assuming additional risk. Lower returns should be expected when lower risk levels are assumed.

If you look at two investments, each with 15 percent average annual returns for the past three years, one by investing in blue chip U.S. stocks and the other by investing in pork belly futures, which do you think had the best "risk-adjusted" performance? If you took on more risk by investing in the pork bellies but only experienced the same return as the lower-risk blue chip stocks, it was not a "good" investment since there was no additional compensation for the extra risk taken.

You can measure the degree of risk in a number of ways. Some of the commonly used measurements of risk-related factors include the following:

- Standard deviation — measures the average variability of past returns

- Sharpe ratio — measures risk-adjusted returns

- Treynor index — measures systematic risk in the context of market returns

- Alpha — measures management capability, adjusted for risk

- Beta — measures relative market volatility

- R squared — measures the correlation of the investment to the overall market

- Duration — measures interest-rate risk for fixed-income investments

- Bond quality — various rating agencies will rate the credit quality of fixed-income instruments

5. **Actual performance ratios.** Make sure the actual returns are calculated according to AIMR (Association of Investment Management and Research) standards. AIMR standards require calculating returns on a time-weighted return basis. It is also important to calculate returns on a dollar-weighted basis to determine the actual return of the portfolio. The time-weighted return is not influenced by cash inflows or outflows from the portfolio, so it more fairly presents the returns based upon the manager's decisions. In contrast, the dollar-weighted return

takes into account cash flows, giving the internal rate of return. This gives a picture of how well the portfolio has benefited from investment performance over time.

6. **Returns: gross and net of fees.** Report returns on both a gross basis and net of any and all advisor fees.

7. **Other questions to ask the prospective fund or investment manager include:**

- What is your method of compensation? Look for rewards based upon long-term returns, not just end-of-quarter performance. Rewarding short-term performance can cause a manager to take more risk than might be appropriate to boost end-of-quarter returns.

- What is the research process and the investment purchase/sale decision-making process?

- Who will make the investment decisions? Is it the same person or group responsible for creating the past performance of the investment?

- What is the unique and defining aspect of the investment strategy?

- Are "soft dollar" concessions received by the manager for trades in your account credited against the fees you are charged?

- What is the ownership form of the firm, size of staff and tenure of managers?

- Are derivatives used in the portfolio, and if so, how and why?

- What does the investment manager do to ensure and monitor "best execution" for trades?

- How much turnover has the investment experienced in the past?

- Has it been consistent? If it has changed, why?

- What kind of cash balances does the manager typically keep and is there a strategy for its use?

- What are the investment expenses and are they in line with their peers? Expenses to be reviewed should include:

  — Custodial

  — Investment manager

  — Consulting

  — Brokerage, transaction charges, and markups

  — Other "soft costs"

8. **Fiduciaries are responsible for overseeing the investments.** They also incur other costs that must be controlled. Expenses you need to periodically review for appropriateness include:

- Legal

- Accounting

- Administrative

- Actuarial

- Brokerage commissions

- Investment management

Duties and Responsibilities of the Money Managers

Ideally, each investment or money manager would be informed about and adhere to the Investment Policy Statement objectives and guidelines set forth, and each one would agree in writing to the guidelines. If deviations are permitted, the agreement should clearly state under what circumstances they would be allowed.

Money managers will generally be given discretionary power over investments under their control. While separate account managers may be reluctant to formally acknowledge the policy agreement you have with your client, if you as the advisor are responsible for the manager investing a portion of your client's portfolio in a stated way, how will you be able to be sure it happens?

Such managers should be required to notify the investor in writing if there are any significant or material issues or changes pertaining to the investments, including but not limited to:

1. Investment strategy

2. Portfolio structure

3. Tactical approaches

4. Ownership or organization structure of the money management firm

5. Financial condition

6. Professional staff

7. Recommendation for changes in the investment guidelines

8. Any legal or regulatory issues potentially affecting the investments

The agreement should specify the process for handling proxy votes.

Managers should be required to acknowledge and agree in writing as to their fiduciary status and responsibility to the investor.

Money managers should be required to seek the best price and execution available for each transaction, and should keep records indicating compliance.

If the financial advisor is selecting mutual funds, it is the advisor's responsibility to select and monitor according to all of these conditions.

Monitoring the Investments

Now that time and effort have been put into to developing the Investment Policy Statement, the work is not over. The process of monitoring the activities of all the parties involved must begin.

The basis for monitoring investment managers is essentially the same as that outlined in the selection process described above. The same criteria for selection can be used for monitoring. How frequently this information is reviewed should be identified in the

Investment Policy Statement (it should be reviewed at least once a year, preferably more frequently).

Guidelines for putting a poorly performing investment or manager on "probation" should also be determined. Just because a manager has one bad quarter or year does not mean that manager should be dismissed. It is more common to put such a manager on some kind of "watch list" for a period of time to determine if he or she is still meeting the criteria for retention. Wording for the probation guidelines might include something like the following:

In the event any selected fund underperforms the applicable averages for a period of three years, the selected fund will be placed on probation for the subsequent 12 months. If over the subsequent year the fund's average return for applicable three-year period remains below that earned by the average equivalent pooled investment vehicle sharing the same investment objective, the Advisor, in conjunction with the Investor, will make a determination as to whether the fund continues to be a prudent and appropriate investment.

The relative risk of the selected investment vehicle will also be reviewed on a quarterly basis, as measured by the funds' standard deviation, over the most recent one-, three-, and five-year periods. The fund's relative risk is to be calculated by independent fund evaluation services such as Lipper Analytical Services, Inc., CDA or Morningstar, Inc. In the event the level of risk assumed by the fund exceeds that incurred by the average for equivalent pooled investment vehicles sharing the same investment objective by more than 20 percent over any previous three-year period, the Advisor, in conjunction with the Investor, will make a determination as to whether the fund continues to be a prudent and appropriate investment.

Control Procedures

The Investment Policy Statement should identify how frequently reporting, information and calculations need to be submitted by the advisors to the fiduciaries or decision makers.

Virtually all of the information that has been described above should be periodically reviewed and reported to the fiduciaries. In fact, the Investment Policy Statement itself should be updated at least annually. Whenever there are new economic outlooks, new cash-flow projections, new investor information, perhaps new investment objectives or asset allocation targets, or updated information on investment managers, the Investment Policy Statement should be modified to reflect these new circumstances. It is especially useful to have this information reported side-by-side with the prior year's comparable information when such modifications are made.

6. Signatures

While the IPS is not a legal document, it is important. Asking for signatures signals that importance. Once signed by both the investor ("Yes, this is how I want my money managed") and the advisor (acknowledging the investor's wishes), then implementation can begin.

Guidelines for Working with Qualified Plans

T HERE ARE CERTAIN GUIDELINES that advisors who work with qualified retirement plans must follow. The Department of Labor (DOL) is charged with overseeing these plans and making sure that plan participants are being reasonably served. Their guidelines for fiduciaries include, but are certainly not limited to:

1. **Recommend proper investments**
   The advisor is expected to apply acceptable due diligence procedures before recommending any investment. Investments must meet the overall requirements of the plan.

2. **Diversify plan assets sufficiently to minimize risk**
   Avoid high concentrations in any asset category. The burden of proof falls on the fiduciaries to show how they were being prudent when such a concentration exists.

3. **Monitor liquidity requirements of the plan and maintain adequate amounts**

   Company plans need to be able to make their required payments when employees leave or are terminated. In some cases, this can represent a significant portion of the plan assets. With that in mind, a flow of funds projection is needed and should be kept up to date for monitoring purposes. This should include expected contributions and distributions over the next one, three and five years. Such projections should be part of the plan records.

4. **Achieve reasonable returns for the plan assets**

   Fiduciaries are expected to make an appropriate effort to obtain reasonable returns on the supervised assets, without taking excessive risks. One interpretation of this guideline: It is "the fiduciary duty to maximize return for fund beneficiaries ..." — *former Treasury Secretary Nicholas Brady*

5. **Help control investment expenses**

   Unnecessary and excessive expenses cut directly into the returns provided to the plan participants. It is therefore a vital role of the fiduciaries to monitor and control expenses.

6. **Be prepared for and encourage careful and prudent inspections of advisory background and qualifications**

   Investment managers must be selected with care and appropriate due diligence by plan trustees. Investment advisors or their firms must be registered with the Securities and Exchange Commission or with the state. They should have the related education and experience to clearly be able to offer appropriate guidance to plan trustees. Trustees are also encouraged to check on personal references and investment track records.

7. **Investment advisors are expected to provide to the plan trustees regular investment activity reports and updated performance information**

   Investment manager performance must be monitored and supervised. Unless trustees are regularly informed of the activities and results of their investment managers, they cannot provide the appropriate degree of supervision. Advisors to the trustees should encourage regular discussions of both absolute and relative performance results and the strategy for future decisions. All rate of return figures should be based on time-weighted averages.

8. **Maintain records of all meetings and decisions**

   Written evidence of consistent supervision and evaluation of investment programs must be maintained. The reports that the advisor prepares for the trustees should be maintained as a permanent record to show that the investment management is being properly monitored.

   Most people who run small companies have little free time. One of the important services the advisor can provide is the recording of discussions and decisions. These "minutes" can be kept directly or summarized in a follow-up letter. Either way, this helps meet an important requirement.

9. **Know the client's goals and attitudes**

   Every advisor working with investments should have an investment questionnaire that identifies the client's attitudes regarding risk and volatility, required rates of return, restricted investments, preferences for issues such as socially responsible investing, etc. Such a questionnaire, when constructed properly, not only can elicit crucial information about the client, but can also serve as an important teaching tool. Clients cannot be properly served without a clear understanding of their investment attitudes.

10. **Asset valuation must be done with care and any problems should be fully disclosed.**

    Partnership investments are particularly troublesome in this regard. When vested benefits are paid out to terminating employees, too high a valuation favors the departing employee and works against the remaining participants. Too low a valuation produces the opposite result. In either case, disgruntled participants can complain to the DOL. This makes it incumbent upon the advisor to discuss the issues with the plan trustees and fully disclose all the facts and considerations.

11. **Meet with plan participants periodically**

    Employees have a right to a reasonable understanding of their benefit programs. Most employers will appreciate the advisor's help in explaining how the program works and how it can best benefit each employee, thus probably raising the level of participation. Some advisors make it a policy to not only meet with employees as a group, but to also require a one-to-one meeting with each participant. This will allow the advisor to personalize the explanation and it offers the opportunity to develop new client relationships.

12. **Provide plan trustees annually with ADV Part II**

    Plan trustees must know from whom they are receiving advice and are therefore required to ask for this information.

13. **Maintain appropriate ERISA bonding**

    All fiduciaries, including investment advisors, must carry an ERISA bond. This coverage must exceed 10 percent of the value of the plan assets. Such coverage can be obtained from many property and casualty brokers or brokers specializing in such coverage.

14. **Don't participate in prohibited transactions**

    Prohibited transactions are generally those dealings that involve a potential conflict of interest or that unduly benefit a fiduciary or "party in interest." Since most advisors will be considered fiduciaries to their plan clients, and in virtually all cases will be "parties in interest," avoiding prohibited transactions becomes especially noteworthy.

Prohibited transactions of particular note include:

1) Sale, exchange or lease of any personal property to the plan

2) Loans or other extensions of credit

3) Furnishing goods, other services or facilities

4) Transfers to or use of any plan assets

5) Any fiduciary self-dealing, such as:

   a) Acting on both sides of a transaction, such as the sale/purchase of a limited partnership interest, in which a plan client is involved

   b) Kickbacks paid as a result of recommending the purchase of a product

15. **Don't expose plan assets to excessive risk, but don't avoid risk either**

    Plan trustees are not asked by the law to entirely eliminate risk. (After all, the pursuit of attractive returns, by definition, involves some risk.) Rather, trustees are asked only to make their decisions in a systematic manner appropriate to one who understands modern investment practices. Courts have consistently avoided finding fault, despite any losses, if the fiduciaries had followed prudent procedures in making their investment decisions. Blame will generally be found only where the process itself was faulty.

    Problems may also arise when the DOL finds that the achieved rates of return are not commensurate with the level of risk involved.

Summary:

Due to the complexity of ERISA and the potential severe penalties, the qualified plan arena is not a field to embark upon without expertise. Consistent use of the do's and don'ts listed here will help the advisor serve the best interests of the ERISA client and will help keep everyone out of trouble.

ERISA Compliance Quick Checklist

Compliance with the Employee Retirement Income Security Act (ERISA) begins with knowing the rules. Plan administrators and other plan officials can use this checklist as a quick diagnostic tool for assessing a plan's compliance with certain important ERISA rules; it is not a complete description of all ERISA rules and it is not a substitute for a comprehensive compliance review. Use of this checklist is voluntary, and it should not be filed with your Form 5500.

If you answer "No" to any of the questions below, you should review your plan's operations because you may not be in full compliance with ERISA requirements.

1. Have you provided plan participants with a summary plan description, summaries of any material modifications of the plan, and annual summary financial reports?

2. Do you maintain copies of plan documents at the principal office of the plan administrator for examination by participants and beneficiaries?

3. Do you respond to written participant inquires for copies of plan documents and information within 30 days?

4. Does your plan include written procedures for making benefit claims and appealing denied claims, and are you complying with those procedures?

5. Is your plan covered by a fidelity bond against losses due to fraud or dishonesty?

6. Are the plan's investments diversified so as to minimize the risk of large losses?

7. If the plan permits participants to select the investments in their plan accounts, has the plan provided them with enough information to make informed decisions?

8. Has a plan official determined that the investments are prudent and solely in the interest of the plan's participants and beneficiaries, and evaluated the risks associated with plan investments before making the investments?

9. Did the employer or other plan sponsor send participant contributions to the plan on a timely basis?

10. Did the plan pay participant benefits on time and in the correct amounts?

If you answer "Yes" to any of the questions below, you should review your plan's operations because you may not be in full compliance with ERISA requirements.

1. Has the plan engaged in any financial transactions with persons related to the plan or any plan official—for example, has the plan made a loan to or participated in an investment with the employer?

2. Has the plan official used the assets of the plan for his or her own interest?

3. Have plan assets been used to pay expenses that were not authorized in the plan document, were not necessary to the proper administration of the plan, or were more than reasonable in amount?

If you need help answering these questions or want additional guidance about ERISA requirements, a plan official should contact the U.S. Department of Labor Pension and Welfare Benefits Administration office in your region or consult with the plan's legal counsel or professional employee benefit advisor.

---

* Source: U.S. Department of Labor

Conclusion

I N CONCLUSION, we believe it is important for the advisor to remember that (1) it is bad practice not to have a written policy statement; (2) it is worse if you have one and don't follow it. Therefore, as you develop and document your investment policies with the client, make sure that the policies you are recording are ones that you can and will adhere to. For example: if you document your investment selection process, don't later decide to make changes in your procedures or your criteria, unless you also change the policy statement. A key to success, then, is writing the policy in such a way that you expect to be able to live with it for quite a while.

As you develop and document your investment policies with the client, make sure that the policies you are recording are ones that you can and will adhere to.

Making investment decisions or helping others make investment decisions have their own unique challenges and responsibilities. A systematic process, such as the one we have described, permits you to satisfy the special responsibilities of financial fiduciaries and address these challenges.

The goal of the Investment Policy Statement should be to clearly identify:

- Investment goals

- How the goals will be achieved

- The discipline that will allow the investment plan to stay on track

The key is to remember that with fiduciary responsibility, it is the integrity of the process that is most important, not the results of any individual decision.

Best wishes for your success in this endeavor. Please feel free to call on either of us if we can be of any assistance or if you have any suggestions about how we can improve this guidebook.

Linda S. Lubitz, CFP*

Norman M. Boone, MBA, CFP*

www.InvestmentPolicyStatement.com

Suggested Readings

Procedural Prudence and Fiduciary Responsibility

Managing Pension Assets: Pension Finance and Corporate Goals
Walter R. Good and Douglas A. Love
McGraw Hill Publishing, 1990

The Management of Investment Decisions
Donald B. Trone, William Albright
and William Madden
Irwin Professional Publishing, 1995

Fiduciary Responsibility under ERISA: Where Does It Begin? Where Does It End?
Russell A. Gauderies, Jr. and
Robert C. Macula, Jr.
ALA-ABA Course Materials Journal

The New York Prudent Investor Act: Focus on Tax Considerations
Arthur M. Sherwood
New York State Bar Journal, November 1994

Common Mistakes of Fiduciaries Responsible for Investments
Lynn Hopewell, The Monitor Group
The Journal of Investing, Winter 1994

Investment Policy Guidebook for Corporate Pension Plan Trustees
Special Committee of the International Foundation of Employee Benefit Plans
IFEBP, 1990

Fiduciary Responsibility in Retirement Plans
Norman M. Boone, MBA, CFP*
Personal Financial Planning, May 1991

Developing the Investment Policy Statement
Norman M. Boone, MBA, CFP*, and
Linda S. Lubitz, CFP*
Journal of Financial Planning, April 1992

A Review of Difficult Investment Policy Issues
Norman M. Boone, MBA, CFP*, and
Linda S. Lubitz, CFP*
Journal of Financial Planning, May 2003

Global Investing

Global Investing: The Professional's Guide to the World Capital Markets
Roger G. Ibbotson and G.P. Brinson
McGraw-Hill, 1993

Quantitative International Investing
Brian R. Bruce
Probes Publishing Co., 1990

The World Market Wealth Portfolio
Journal of Portfolio Management, Winter 1983

Investment (Asset) Valuation

How to Forecast Long-run Asset Returns
Roger G. Ibbotson and Laurence B. Siegel,
Ibbotson Associates
Investment Management Review,
September-October 1988

Investment: Concepts-Analysis-Strategy
R.C. Radcliff
Third Edition
HarperCollins, 1990

State of the Art in Estimating the Cost of Capital
Laurence B. Siegel, Ibbotson Associates
Chief Financial Officer USA, 1988,
pp. 71–74

The Performance of Real Estate as an Asset Class
Roger G. Ibbotson and W. N. Goetz Mann
Journal of Applied Corporate Finance

Asset Allocation

Asset Allocation: A Multi-Economic Scenario Approach
William Doberman
Journal of Financial Planning, October 1993

Asset Allocation: Balancing Financial Risk
Roger C. Gibson
The McGraw Hill Companies, 1990, 1996, 2000

Asset Allocation for the Individual Investor
Institute of Chartered Financial Analysts, 1987

Diversify: The Investor's Guide to Asset Allocation Strategies
Gerald W. Parrott and Alan Levine
Longman Financial Services Publishing, 1990

Mean-Variance Optimization

Active Asset Allocation: Gaining Advantage in a Highly Efficient Stock Market
W.G. Good, R.W. Hormones and J.R. Meyer
McGraw-Hill, 1993

Active Asset Allocation: State-of-the-Art Portfolio Policies, Strategies, and Tactics
R.D. Arnett and F.J. Abuzz
Probus Publishing Co., 1992

Asset Allocation: Balancing Financial Risk
Chapters 9–11: Portfolio Optimization, Knowing Your Clients, Managing Client Expectations
Roger C. Gibson
The McGraw Hill Companies, 1990, 1996, 2000

Portfolio Selection:
Efficient Diversification of Investments
H.M. Markowitz
John Wiley & Sons, 1959

Stocks, Bonds, Bills, and Inflation Yearbook
Chapter 9: Using Historical Data in Optimization and Forecasting
Roger G. lbbotson and Rex A. Sinquefield
© Ibbotson Associates

Taming Your Optimizer: A Guide Through the Pitfalls of Mean-Variance Optimization
Excerpts from Advances in Asset Allocation
Scott L. Lummer, Mark W. Riepe and Laurence B. Siegel, lbbotson Associates
John Wiley & Sons, 1990

Portfolio Management

A Random Walk Down Wall Street
B.G. Malkiel
W.W. Norton, 1973

Determinants of Portfolio Performance
G.P. Brinson, L.R. Hood, and G.L. Beebower
Financial Analysts Journal, July-August 1986
Updated by:
G.P. Brinson, B.D. Singer and G.L. Beebower
Financial Analysts Journal, May-June 1991

How to Invest Someone Else's Money
J.W. Guy, CFP*
Richard D. Irwin, Inc., 1994

Investment Analysis and Portfolio Management
Chapter 4: Development of Modern Portfolio Theory
J.B. Cohen, E.D. Zinbarg and A. Zeikel
Fifth Edition
Richard D. Irwin, Inc., 1987

Investment Markets:
Gaining the Performance Advantage
Roger G. lbbotson and G.P. Brinson
McGraw-Hill, 1987

Investment Policy—
How to Win the Loser's Game
Charles Ellis
by Dow Jones Irwin, 1985

Wealth Management
Harold Evensky
Richard D. Irwin, Inc., 1997

Security Analysis

Financial Markets and the Economy
C.N. Henning, W. Pigott and R.H. Scott
Prentice Hall, 1988

Historical U.S. Treasury Yield Curves
Roger G. Ibbotson, T.S. Coleman and L. Fisher
Ibbotson Associates, 1993

Security Analysis: Principles and Techniques
S. Cottle, D. Dodd and B. Graham
Fourth Edition
McGraw-Hill, 1962

Statistics

Statistics for Business and Economics
P. Newbold
Prentice Hall, 1988

Attribution

Asset Allocation: Management Style and
Performance Measurement
William F. Sharpe
Journal of Portfolio Management, Winter 1992

Factor Analysis: Beyond Indexing
Robert N. Veres
Investment Advisor, September 1994

Other Tools to Help You

Software to help you create an effective IPS
Association of Investment Management &
Research (AIMR)

Investment Planning and Policy
published by the Investment Management
Consultants Association, Denver, CO

Investment Policy: Winning the Losers Game
Charles Ellis, Irwin Publishing

Measuring Risk & Managing Client
Expectations
Practitioners Publishing Company
(800) 323-8724

The Moneymax® Personal Profiling System
Kathleen Gurney
(800) 735-7935

Sample Risk Tolerance Questionnaire

The questionnaire in this Appendix is a representative one that we use with our clients. It contains much of the information needed to complete the IPS for the client. Most advisors have developed their own documents that are used to gather information about the client.

Investment Policy & Risk Tolerance

Discussion Guide and Questionnaire

Client Name: _____

Co-Client Name: _____

Advisor Name: _____

Date: _____

BOONE FINANCIAL ADVISORS INC.

Helping You Shape Your Financial Future

433 California Street, Suite 520
San Francisco, CA 94104
415/788-1952
fax: 415/788-7105
www.BooneAdvisors.com
info@BooneAdvisors.com

Documents We Will Need from You

If we do not already have them, we will need the following from you:

Federal Tax Return
- Most recent

Investment Statements (Your most recent copy)
- Investment Brokerage Accounts
- Investment Accounts
- Stock Option Grants
- Company Stock
- Employee Stock Purchase or ESOP
- Mutual Funds
- Bank Accounts
- Money Market Accounts
- Partnerships (K-1 report, if you don't have anything else)
- Others

Retirement Account Statements
- IRA(s)
- Keogh
- SEP
- 401(k)
- 403(b)
- 457
- Other Company Retirement Accounts
  — Profit Sharing Plan
  — Money Purchase Plan
  — Defined Benefit Plan

College Funding Account Statements
- UTMA
- 529 State College Savings
- Coverdell Education Savings Account

Client Information

Personal Information

Last Name _____ Last Name _____

First Name _____ First Name _____

Gender _____ Date of Birth (mm/dd/yy) _____   Gender _____ Date of Birth (mm/dd/yy) _____

Social Security Number _____ Social Security Number _____

Work Phone # _____ Work Phone # _____

Work Fax # _____ Work Fax # _____

Cell Phone # _____ Cell Phone # _____

Email _____ Email _____

Home Address _____

City _____ State _____ Zip _____ Country _____

Home Phone # _____ Home Fax # _____

Name of Child or Dependent	Gender	School Grade (if any)	Age	Child's Parent (Both/Father/Mother)	Date of Birth
				B F M	
				B F M	
				B F M	
				B F M	
				B F M	
				B F M	

Background Information

What is your total household annual income and tax bracket?

	Household Income	Tax Bracket
Last year	$	%
Expected this year	$	%
Expected next year	$	%

How do you expect your income to change in the future?

_____

_____

How much did you save (or withdraw) during the years identified in each of the following?

	Household Income Taxable Accounts	Client Retirement Accounts	Co-Client Retirement Accounts
Last year	$	$	$
Expected this year	$	$	$
Expected next year	$	$	$

How do you expect your savings/withdrawal pattern to change in the future?

_____

_____

What is the approximate value of the assets in the investment portfolio you are considering having us manage?

$_____

What percentage of your total investments does this portfolio represent?

_____%

Your Investment Objectives

1. Please describe your investment goals/objectives.

_____

_____

_____

_____

_____

2. Are you satisfied with the way in which you are accomplishing your investment goals?

☐ Yes ☐ No   Please explain:

_____

_____

_____

_____

_____

3. What is your primary objective for this investment portfolio?
(check one)

☐ To ensure the safety of my principal

☐ To generate income. If so, how much will you need annually? $_____

☐ To achieve a particular investment goal. If so, what goal(s)?

_____

☐ To accumulate assets for retirement

☐ Other. Please explain:

_____

4. Ranking Objectives

Most of us have several objectives relating to our investments. Please choose among the following objectives, assigning them points (the more points assigned, the more important you think the priority is). The points should total 100.

Safety/Capital Preservation	_____	Points
Capital Appreciation	_____	Points
Liquidity	_____	Points
Inflation Protection	_____	Points
Current Income	_____	Points
Tax Shelter	_____	Points
Total	100	

5. Do you expect to have a need for income from this portfolio within five years?

☐ Yes ☐ No

If yes, when will the income or withdrawal be needed?   In _____ years.

6. Will significant deposits or withdrawals be made over the next five years?

☐ Yes ☐ No

If yes, please attach a listing of their anticipated amount and timing.

7. Return Targets

Given the fact that over the long run (from 1927 to 200X), U.S. stocks have generated historical returns of about 10–13 percent, U.S. bonds have returned 5–6 percent, money markets have returned 3–4 percent and U.S. inflation has been approximately 3 percent, what do you expect the total return of your investment portfolio to be over the long term? (check one)

☐ 3–5%   ☐ 6–7%   ☐ 8–9%   ☐ 10–11%   ☐ 12–14%   ☐ more than 15%

8. What is your investment time horizon for this portfolio?

"Investment time horizon" refers to the number of years you expect the portfolio to be invested before you make substantial withdrawals from the portfolio. Alternatively, how long will the objectives stated for this portfolio continue without substantial modification? Please mark your choice:

☐ 3 years ☐ 5 years ☐ 10 years ☐ More than 10 years

9. **Do you have any "socially responsible" concerns or issues that you would like to see manifested in your portfolio?**
If so, please describe.

_____

_____

10. **What tax considerations would you like us to keep in mind in managing your portfolio?**

☐ If possible, I would like to reduce the current level of tax I pay.

☐ I would like to better control my future taxable distributions and income.

☐ I have unused tax losses available.

☐ Tax management of my investment portfolio is not a concern.

Your Tolerance for Risk

Your comfort level with investment risk influences how aggressively or conservatively you choose to invest. It should be balanced with the potential of achieving your investment goals.

11. **How would your describe your knowledge of investments?**
(check one)

☐ None ☐ Limited ☐ Good ☐ Extensive

12. **What is your investment temperament?** (check one)

☐ I am more interested in conserving capital than growth. I prefer to accept moderate income and little or no growth in exchange for stability and minimum risk.

☐ I understand that to achieve higher returns, it is necessary to take some risk. I am willing to accept moderate volatility in the value of my portfolio in exchange for greater income and/or growth potential.

147

☐ I understand that to achieve higher returns, it is necessary to take some risk. I am willing to be more aggressive and face greater risk in order to pursue the possibility of above-average rates of return.

13. **An investment decision involves the possibility of high return as well as the possibility of suffering a loss. What most influences your thinking when making an important investment decision?** (check one)

☐ I'm mainly influenced by the potential gain.

☐ I'm more influenced by the potential gain than by the potential loss.

☐ I'm more influenced by the potential loss than by the potential gain.

☐ I'm mainly influenced by the potential loss.

14. **Which of the following statements best describes what your reaction would be to short-term fluctuations in this investment portfolio?**

☐ I would be extremely uneasy about any fluctuations in the value of my investment.

☐ I would be very concerned about short-term fluctuations in the value of my investment.

☐ I would have some worries about short-term fluctuations in the value of my investment.

☐ I would have very little concern about short-term fluctuations in the value of my investment.

15. **Imagine that the stock market has dropped 20 percent in value over the last year. A stock or mutual fund that you own has also dropped 20 percent in value. What is your reaction?** (check one)

☐ Sell all my shares

☐ Sell some of my shares

☐ Keep all my shares

☐ Keep all my shares and buy more shares

16. **Please check the statement that reflects your preference.** (check one)

☐ I would rather be out of the stock market when it goes down than in the market when it goes up (i.e., I cannot live with the volatility of the stock market).

☐ I would rather be in the stock market when it goes down than out of the market when it goes up (i.e., I may not like the idea, but I can live with the volatility of the stock market in order to earn market returns.)

17. **If you could increase your chances of having a more comfortable retirement by taking more risk, would you**

☐ Be unlikely to take much more risk?

☐ Be willing to take a little more risk with some of your money?

☐ Be willing to take a little more risk with all of your money?

☐ Be willing to take a lot more risk with all of your money?

18. **Except for the Great Depression, the longest time investors have had to wait after a market crash, or a really bad market decline, for their portfolio to return to its earlier value has been 4 years for stock and 2 years for bond investments. Knowing this, and that it is impossible to protect yourself from an occasional loss if you choose to invest at least some of your portfolio in stocks, please answer the following question:**

If my portfolio is designed to produce a long-term return that should allow me to accomplish my goals, I am prepared to live with a time of recovery of…"

☐ Less than one year.*

☐ Between one and two years.*

☐ Between two and three years.*

☐ Over three years.

*If you select a period of three years or less, are you prepared to substantially reduce your goals? (check one)

☐ Yes ☐ No

19. **The following chart shows the historical range of values for four different investments of $1 million after one year. Which investment would you be most comfortable owning?** (check one)

☐ Investment A   ☐ Investment D

☐ Investment B   ☐ Investment E

☐ Investment C

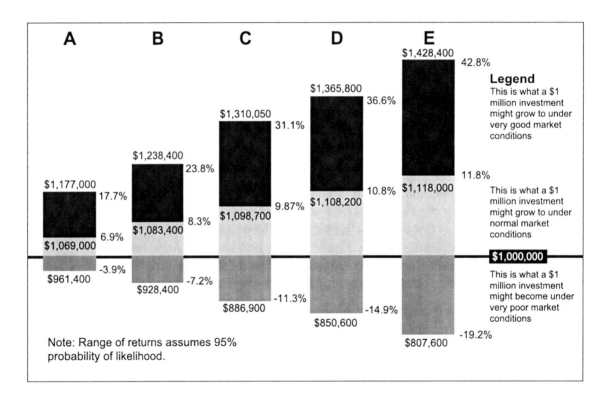

Dealing with Investment Declines

Over the past 75 years (beginning in 1927 and ending in 200X), the U.S. stock market (as measured by the S&P 500 Index) has produced a compound return of 11%. During this time, the annual calendar year return for the U.S. stock market has:

Size of Market Drop	Frequency
Decreased over 30%	2 times
Decreased 20–30%	3 times
Decreased 10–20%	5 times
Decreased 0–10%	13 times
Increased 0–10%	11 times
Increased over 10%	44 times

(data provided by Ibbotson Associates, SBBI 2004 Yearbook)

20. **Given the above information, which statement best reflects your attitude about investing in the U.S. stock market?** (check one)

☐ I am unwilling to experience any reduction in the value of my investments.

☐ I can tolerate infrequent, very limited declines (less than 5%) through difficult phases in a stock market cycle.

☐ I can tolerate limited declines (5–10%) through difficult phases in a stock market cycle.

☐ I can tolerate periods of moderate negative returns (declines of 10–15%) to achieve potentially higher investment returns. I recognize and accept that negative returns could persist for a year and possibly longer.

☐ I can tolerate periods of significant negative returns (greater than 20%) for the chance to maximize my long-term returns. I recognize and accept that negative returns could persist for a year and possibly longer.

21. **To achieve the investment returns you want, how much decline would you be willing to tolerate in a given year in your investment portfolio?**

☐ None   ☐ 0–5%

☐ 5–10%   ☐ 10–15%

☐ 15–20%   ☐ 20+%

151

Your Financial Capacity to take Risk

Your ability to accept risk is not only influenced by your emotional tolerance for risk. The appropriateness of whether or not you should accept more or less risk is also influenced by the relative strength of your personal finances. With that in mind, please rank your current personal financial strength in each of the following areas:

22. Your Financial Capacity to take on risk

Rate each on 1 (weak) to 10 (strong) scale

a. Cash Reserves   a. _____

b. Income Stability   b. _____

c. Cashflow Strength (spending vs. income)   c. _____

d. Insurance Coverage   d. _____

e. Overall Wealth (relative to your needs)   e. _____

f. Fixed Obligations as % of Income   f. _____

Investment Policy Items

23. How would you describe your outlook for your own finances over the next...

	1 Year	5 Years	10 Years
a. Very positive	_____	_____	_____
b. Modestly positive	_____	_____	_____
c. Neutral	_____	_____	_____
d. Modestly negative	_____	_____	_____
e. Very negative	_____	_____	_____
f. I am undecided	_____	_____	_____

24. **What is your outlook on inflation for the next...**

	1 Year	5 Years	10 Years
a. It will increase	‾‾‾‾‾	‾‾‾‾‾	‾‾‾‾‾
b. It will be steady	‾‾‾‾‾	‾‾‾‾‾	‾‾‾‾‾
c. It will decrease	‾‾‾‾‾	‾‾‾‾‾	‾‾‾‾‾

25. **Capital Needs Analysis**

If a capital needs analysis has been performed for you, what rate of return did it indicate will be needed for you to accomplish your goals? _____%

26. **Frequency of Review**

A. Evaluation of how well we managed your portfolio will occur every _____ years.

B. Frequency of review of this IPS will occur every _____ years.

27. **Rebalancing Procedures**

As a "rebalancing trigger" used in the ongoing management of your investment portfolio, we generally consider it time to make changes when any asset class in your portfolio differs from its target allocation by 5% or more.

Please indicate whether or not that is an acceptable approach for your portfolio.

☐ Yes   ☐ No

Boone Financial Advisors, Inc. accepts full discretion to make rebalancing portfolio changes as long as approved policy targets and existing investments are utilized.

Please indicate whether or not that is an acceptable approach for your portfolio

☐ Yes   ☐ No

Prudent investment diversification involves the use of different asset classes in a portfolio (e.g., cash, stocks, bonds). Since each asset class will often react differently to given economic conditions, diversification can lower a portfolio's overall volatility (risk).

28. Investment Constraints

Are there any securities types or classes that you do not want to have in your portfolio or that you would like to impose limits upon? If so, please check the appropriate items below so that we can discuss your concerns further:

ASSET CLASSES

☐ Municipal Bonds

☐ Government or Corporate Bonds

☐ High Yield Bonds

☐ Non-U.S. Bonds

☐ U.S. Equities – Large Companies

☐ U.S. Equities – Small Companies

☐ Foreign Equities –
Developed Country

☐ Foreign Equities – Emerging Market

☐ Real Estate Securities/REITS

☐ Hedge Funds

☐ Commodities

☐ Venture Capital

SECURITIES TYPES

☐ Individual Stocks or Bonds

☐ Open-ended Mutual Funds

☐ Closed-end Mutual Funds

☐ Exchange Traded Funds

☐ Managed Separate Accounts

☐ Investment Partnerships

☐ Futures, Options,
Puts, Short Sales

29. Liquidity

When cash (money market funds, bank CDs, etc.) is kept as part of a portfolio, some people want or need a specific portion to remain as cash, so it can be easily called upon. As part of this investment portfolio you wish to maintain:

☐ No minimum liquidity needs (cash is handled separately).

☐ A minimum of _____% of total investments in cash/cash equivalents.

☐ At least $_____ in cash/cash equivalents.

For how long will these needs apply?

_____

Up to what percent can this portfolio be invested in long term, illiquid investments (in other words ones that could not be quickly turned into cash except at a large sacrifice)?

☐ 0%   ☐ 10%   ☐ 20%   ☐ 30%   ☐ 40%

30. Other Investment Considerations (optional)

A. Maximum average bond maturities	No more than _____ years
B. Maximum individual bond maturity	No more than _____ years
C. Maximum portion of portfolio in a single fund	No more than _____ %
D. Maximum portion of portfolio in a single security	No more than _____ %
E. Management style	☐ Passive
	☐ Active
	☐ Combination
	☐ No preference

31. Frequency of Meetings

How frequently would you like to meet with us to discuss your investments?

☐ Quarterly   ☐ Semi-annually   ☐ Annually

The analysis and recommendations we will develop for you are specifically tailored to your situation and their appropriateness is dependent upon the accuracy of the information you provide in this questionnaire.

Signatures:

_____   _____
              Client   Date

_____   _____
            Co-client   Date

Sample
IPS Documents

- Template for the Individual/Married Client
- Template for a Family Trust Client
- Template for the Charitable Remainder Trust Client
- Template for the Endowment or Foundation Client
- Template for the Pension Plan Client
- Template for the Profit Sharing Client
- Template for the 401(k) Client
- Template for the Insurance Trust Client

We are giving the reader a variety of template styles and formats that we have used for various clients. The reader should understand that these templates are for illustrative purposes and the asset allocation, historical return data and client situations are fictional. There are differences between each template which can or cannot be incorporated in the others depending upon the advisor's preferences.

All risk and return numbers provided in the templates are for illustrative purposes only. The reader should not use these sample numbers in real documents for your clients.

Investment Policy Statement

Joseph and Mary Wimbush

August 15, 200X

Wee Manage Money

Basement
Very Small Building
Little Town, CO 30300
303-303-3003

Table of Contents

Introduction

The purpose of this Investment Policy Statement (IPS) is to establish a clear understanding between Joseph and Mary Wimbush ("Investor") and Wee Manage Money ("Advisor") as to the investment goals and objectives and management policies applicable to the Investor's investment portfolio ("Portfolio"). This Investment Policy Statement:

- Establishes the Investor's expectations, objectives and guidelines in the investment of the Portfolio's assets

- Creates the framework for a well-diversified asset mix that can be expected to generate acceptable long-term returns at a level of risk suitable to the Investor, including:

  — describing an appropriate risk posture for the investment of the Investor's Portfolio

  — specifying the target asset allocation policy

  — establishing investment guidelines regarding the selection of investment managers, permissible securities and diversification of assets

  — specifying the criteria for evaluating the performance of the Portfolio's assets

- Defines the responsibilities of the Investor and the Advisor

- Encourages effective communication between the investment manager(s) and the Investor

This IPS is not a contract. No legal counsel has reviewed this investment policy and the Advisor and Investor use it at their own discretion. This IPS is intended to be a summary of an investment philosophy and the procedures that provide guidance for the Investor and the Advisor. The investment policies described in this IPS should be dynamic. These policies should reflect the Investor's current status and philosophy regarding the investment of the Portfolio. These policies will be reviewed and revised periodically to ensure they adequately reflect any changes related to the Portfolio, to the Investor or the capital markets.

It is understood that there can be no guarantee about the attainment of the goals or investment objectives outlined herein.

Investment Policy Background

What Is an Investment Policy Statement?

An investment policy outlines and prescribes a prudent and acceptable investment philosophy and defines the investment management procedures and long-term goals for the Investor.

The Need for a Written Policy

The principal reason for developing a long-term investment policy and for putting it in writing is to enable you and us to protect your portfolio from ad hoc revisions of sound long-term policy. Without an investment policy, in times of market turmoil, investors may be inclined to make ad hoc investment decisions that are inconsistent with prudent investment management principles. Your investment policy provides a well-thought-out framework from which sound investment decisions can be made.

The development of an investment policy follows the basic approach underlying financial planning: assessing your financial condition, setting goals, developing a strategy to meet the goals, implementing the strategy, regularly reviewing the results and adjusting the strategy or the implementation as circumstances dictate. In following an investment policy, you'll employ a more disciplined and systematic approach and thereby increase the probability of satisfying your investment goals.

The Uniform Prudent Investor Act ("UPIA") was approved for use in all states at the 1994 annual Conference of Commissioners on Uniform

State Law and by the American Bar Association in 1995. The act provides excellent guidance about the "prudent investment process."

Key provisions of the UPIA include:

- No investment is inherently prudent or imprudent, except in how its inclusion or exclusion impacts the portfolio as a whole.

- Trustees are expected to use all reasonably available strategies to improve the risk/reward relationship of the portfolio.

- Under most circumstances, the assets of the trust must be diversified.

- Trustees are obliged to spread portfolio investments across asset classes to enhance performance and reduce risk.

- The possible effect of inflation must be considered as part of the investment strategy. As a result, use of equities is encouraged to allow the possibility that the portfolio's growth will outpace inflation.

- Fiduciaries have a duty to either demonstrate investment skill in managing trust assets or to delegate investment management to another, more qualified party.

Steps to Take to Establish an Investment Policy

1. Assess your financial situation—identify your goals and your needs

2. Determine your tolerance for risk and your time horizon

3. Develop clear objectives for the portfolio

4. State how the investments are expected to help meet the portfolio objectives

5. Identify any restrictions on the portfolio and its assets

6. Determine the asset classes and mix appropriate (the "Asset Allocation") to maximize the likelihood of achieving the investment objectives at the lowest level of risk

7. Determine the investment methodology to be used with regard to investment (manager) selection, rebalancing, buy-sell disciplines, portfolio reviews and reporting, etc.

8. Implement the decisions

9. Document all investment decisions

The net effect of the written policy is to increase the likelihood that the portfolio will be able to meet the financial needs of the Investor.

Overview Commentary

Account Information

Acct. Title	Acct. Number	Approx. Value
Joint Trust	_____	$663,040
His Individual	_____	$89,003
His IRA Rollover	_____	$160,298
Her IRA Rollover	_____	$4,768
1 Child's UTMA	_____	$54,712
2 Child's UTMA	_____	$71,253
TOTAL		**$1,043,074**

Other Information

Custodian . . . . Charles Schwab & Co.
All assets to be held at the Custodian

Tax ID Number
His 999-99-9999
Hers 888-88-8888

Investment Advisor . . . . Wee Manage Money
Basement, Very Small Building
Little Town, CO 30300
303-303-3003

Other Key Advisors
Attorney . . . . John Q. Courtroom
CPA . . . . Sally Regulation

Investor Circumstances

The Wimbushes are in their mid-40s. She is an independent economic consultant and he is a partner in a commercial real estate firm. Both plan to work for another ten years before they consider retiring. They have two children, ages 8 and 10, for whom they have established UTMA accounts for the purpose of paying for college costs. They are considering 529 plan contributions to supplement the UTMAs.

Recently, they began working with another financial advisor regarding their investments. The results have not been satisfying and they are looking to recover the situation.

Investor's income is excellent but is volatile from year to year, reflecting the general economy. Investor estimates an average annual income of $300,000, ranging from $175,000 to $450,000, until they retire.

The Wimbushes expect inflation will be roughly the same for the next year and then trend upward over the following few years. They have modestly positive future expectations of the economy as a whole.

Investment Philosophy

The basic tenets under which this portfolio will be managed include the following:

1. Modern portfolio theory, as recognized by the 1990 Nobel Prize, will be the philosophical foundation for how the portfolio will be structured and how subsequent decisions will be made. The underlying concepts of modern portfolio theory include:

   - Investors are risk averse. The only acceptable risk is that which is adequately compensated by potential portfolio returns.

   - Markets are efficient. It is virtually impossible to anticipate the future direction of the market as a whole or of any individual security. It is, therefore, unlikely that any portfolio will succeed in consistently "beating the market."

   - The design of the portfolio as a whole is more important than the selection of any particular security within the portfolio. The appropriate allocation of capital among asset classes (stocks, bonds, cash, etc.) will have far more influence on long-term portfolio results than the selection of individual securities. Investing for the long term (preferably longer than ten years) becomes critical to investment success because it allows the long-term characteristics of the asset classes to surface.

   - For a given risk level, an optimal combination of asset classes will maximize returns. Diversification helps reduce investment volatility. The proportional mix of asset classes determines the long-term risk and return characteristics of the portfolio as a whole.

   - Portfolio risk can be decreased by increasing diversification of the portfolio and by lowering the correlation of market behavior among the asset classes selected. (Correlation is the statistical term for the extent to which two asset classes move in tandem or opposition to one another.)

2. Investing globally helps to minimize overall portfolio risk due to the imperfect correlation between economies of the world. Investing globally has also been shown historically to enhance portfolio returns, although there is no guarantee that it will do so in the future.

3. Equities offer the potential for higher long-term investment returns than cash or fixed income investments. Equities are also more volatile in their performance. Investors seeking higher rates of return must increase the proportion of equities in their portfolio, while at the same time accepting greater variation of results (including occasional declines in value).

4. Picking individual securities and timing the purchase or sale of investments in the attempt to "beat the market" are highly unlikely to increase long-term investment returns; they also can significantly increase portfolio operating costs. Such practices are, therefore, to be avoided.

Given these tenets, the underlying approach to managing this portfolio shall be to optimize the risk-return relationship appropriate to Investor's needs and goals. The portfolio will be diversified globally, employing a variety of asset classes. Mutual funds or managed portfolios will be employed to implement the portfolio and the chosen asset classes will be periodically rebalanced to maintain a more consistent risk/reward profile.

Investment Objectives

The overall priorities for the Investor are, respectively, (1) maintaining a comfortable current lifestyle and (2) providing for a comfortable retirement lifestyle. The investor would like to be assured of not running out of money during their lifetime.

A capital needs analysis has been provided by Advisor to determine the appropriate targeted rate of pre-tax average annual investment return (after expenses) for Investor's lifetime. On the basis of that analysis, it currently appears as though a portfolio designed as described in this Investment Policy Statement, should be expected to produce a return of 4.0% above inflation with an 88% probability of successfully meeting their personal and financial goals. Investor was satisfied with that outlook.

Therefore, the long-term objective for the assets under this policy is to achieve a pre-tax average annual return of 4.0% above inflation over the holding period of this portfolio.

Time Horizon

For the purposes of planning, the time horizon for the investments in this portfolio will parallel the combined lifetimes of the Investor. It is assumed that the investment horizon for this portfolio exceeds ten (10) years.

Withdrawals from this portfolio are not expected to begin for approximately seven (7) to ten (10) years. This will most likely be for college funding and subsequently for retirement needs as the earned income is reduced.

Capital values do fluctuate over shorter periods and the Investor recognizes that the possibility of capital loss does exist. However, historical asset class return data suggest that the risk of principal loss over a holding period of at least five years can be minimized with the long-term investment mix employed under this Investment Policy Statement.

Tax Policy

Given Investor's current level of earned income, Investor expects to be in a fairly high marginal federal and state tax bracket for the foreseeable future. Investor has not yet been subject to the alternative minimum tax, but is close enough that exposure to AMT income items should be continually monitored.

Tax-efficient means of investing will be employed where appropriate for Investor's taxable accounts. Such methods may include any of the following: use of low-turnover or passive index mutual and exchange-traded funds, tax-free bonds and funds, active tax loss harvesting and use of lower dividend paying stocks.

The UTMA accounts are currently taxed at Investor's highest marginal tax rates for income in excess of $1500 per year. For that reason, investments held in those accounts will be designed to attempt to maintain taxable income below that level.

Tax-deferred account holdings may be used to hold assets likely to generate higher levels of taxable income, such as taxable bonds and REITs.

Risk Tolerance

There are two primary factors that affect the Investor's risk tolerance:

- Financial capacity to accept risk within the investment program
- Willingness to accept return volatility

Personal Financial Capacity

Investor has good income stability, insurance coverage, liquidity and net worth and plan on adding to their investment portfolio. Investor therefore has considerable financial capacity to take on risk.

Willingness to Tolerate Volatility

Investor also desires long-term investment growth sufficient to meet their objectives. Investor understands that to achieve such growth their portfolio will experience periods of decline. They further understand that in a severe market, the potential recovery period could exceed three years.

Although Investor prefers to limit the portfolio's volatility, Investor indicates a willingness to accept occasional moderate declines in order to position their portfolio for improved growth possibilities. The investor's experiences of the last few years have caused them to think more in terms of safety.

Taking these two factors into account, the Investor's risk tolerance may be characterized as moderately conservative.

Asset Allocation

Academic research offers considerable evidence that the asset allocation decision far outweighs security selection and market timing in its impact on portfolio performance. After reviewing the long-term performance and risk characteristics of various asset classes and balancing the risk and rewards of market behavior, the following asset classes were selected to achieve the objectives of the Investor's Portfolio.

ASSET ALLOCATION

CATEGORY	HOLDINGS	PERCENT	TOTAL
Cash			**1%**
	Money Market Funds	1%	
Bonds			**39%**
	Municipal Bonds	23%	
	Corp./Gov't. Bonds	16%	
	Foreign Bonds		
	High Yield Bonds		
Equities			**55%**
	U.S. Large Stocks	25%	
	U.S. Small Socks	11%	
	International Stocks	15%	
	Emerging Mkt. Stocks	4%	
Real Estate			**5%**
	REITs	5%	
	Direct Ownership		
Alternative Investments			
	Hedge Funds		
	Commodity Funds		
TOTAL		**100%**	**100%**

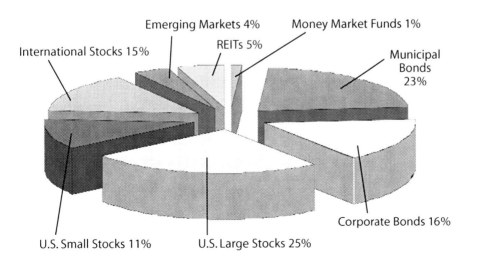

Emerging Markets 4%

International Stocks 15%

REITs 5%

Money Market Funds 1%

Municipal Bonds 23%

Corporate Bonds 16%

U.S. Small Stocks 11%

U.S. Large Stocks 25%

Historical Portfolio Returns & Volatility

The Investor's willingness to accept risk and their expectation for investment growth have a direct bearing on the rate-of-return objective for this portfolio.

The following historical returns reflect the results of this portfolio, as constructed, over the 1972 to 200X time period (30 years).

Bear in mind, these outcomes represent historical results using index data and estimated expenses. It should be recognized that the portfolio will invest in mutual funds or other securities and that the actual weighting of these securities can and will vary. It is also important to note that the future returns of the securities with the portfolio can be expected to vary from the historical returns referenced.

The portfolio results referenced reflect a portfolio design having a "value" orientation (i.e., employing funds or stocks with below-average price-to-book ratios). Historically, over-weighting "value" investments in a portfolio has resulted in higher portfolio returns with lower risk when compared to portfolios with greater "growth" characteristics. The Investor's portfolio will be designed with a "value" orientation.

The portfolio's historical rate of return is not a guarantee of future investment returns. Future returns could differ significantly and capital loss is possible. This Investment Policy Statement shall not be construed as offering a guarantee.

Historical Portfolio & Asset Class Returns (1972 to 200X)

ASSET CLASS	HISTORICAL RETURN	STANDARD DEVIATION
Asset Class Returns (before expenses):		
Cash	6.6%	0.8%
Intermediate Bonds	8.5%	4.9%
U.S. Large Stocks	12.2%	17.5%
U.S. Small Stocks	13.3%	24.8%
International Stocks	11.2%	19.1%
Emerging Market Stocks*	11.3%	27.8%
Real Estate	12.5%	15.4%

* Emerging Market data since 1988

Historical Rolling Period Real Returns (1972 to 200X)

	ROLLING 1-YEAR PERIODS	ROLLING 5-YEAR PERIODS
Annualized Returns:		
Best Period	38.7%	19.2%
Average (arithmetic mean)	4.9%	5.7%
Worst Period	−32.1%	−4.1%
% of Periods Generating:		
Negative returns	29.2%	12.6%
Less than CPI + 4%	49.9%	35.5%
Portfolio Return (geometric mean)	11.4%	10.0%
Less Estimated Expenses	1.7%	
Portfolio Return (net)	9.7%	
Less Inflation (5.0% + 0.3% compounding)	5.3%	1.2%
Real Return After Inflation	4.4%	

The returns reflected above are *after* inflation and include price appreciation, dividends, and interest and are net of 1.7% estimated mutual fund management expenses and advisory fees. They assume use of taxable bonds (municipal bonds yield less but are assumed to return about the same after taxes). Calculations do not include the impact of transaction costs or income taxes.

Updated Allocations

Over time, it may be desirable to amend the basic allocation policy or calculations. When such changes are made, updates will be attached to this Investment Policy Statement as an Appendix and will be considered part of this Investment Policy Statement.

Rebalancing Procedures

From time to time, market conditions may cause the Portfolio's investment in various asset classes to vary from the established allocation. To remain consistent with the asset allocation guidelines established by this Investment Policy Statement, every quarter the Advisor shall review the portfolio and each asset class in which the Portfolio is invested. If the actual weighting differs from the target weighting by 5% or more from the recommended weighting (e.g., from a recommended 10% to less than 5% or more than 15% of total assets) the Advisor shall rebalance the portfolio back to the recommended weighting. Such rebalancing shall be limited to securities previously approved by Investor.

Frequency of Review

The Investor recognizes that all investments go through cycles and, therefore, there will be periods of time in which the investment objectives are not met or when specific managers fail to meet their expected performance expectations.

The Investor accepts the principle that, in the absence of specific circumstances requiring immediate action, patience and a longer-term perspective will be employed when evaluating investment performance.

On an overall portfolio basis, the Investor establishes a goal of evaluating portfolio investment performance relative to investment benchmarks over a minimum period of five years.

The Advisor and the Investor should review this Investment Policy Statement together every two years.

Liquidity

The Investor will maintain adequate liquid reserves outside this portfolio and does not plan on making withdrawals from the portfolio in the immediate future. A minimal allocation to cash will be made for administrative purposes only.

Diversification

Investment of the Investor's funds shall be limited to individual marketable securities or packaged products (for example, mutual funds or unit investment trusts) in the following categories:

Permitted Asset Classes

1. Cash and cash equivalents
2. Fixed income–domestic bonds (including investment grade, high yield and municipal bonds)
3. Fixed income–non-U.S. bonds
4. Equities–U.S.
5. Equities–non-U.S.
6. Equities–emerging markets
7. Equities–REITs
8. Alternative investments

Permitted Security Types

1. Mutual funds–stocks, bonds, money market funds

2. Individual stocks

3. Individual bonds, as long as they are rated A or better and traded on a major U.S. exchange

4. Closed-end funds

5. Unit investment trusts

6. Exchange traded funds

7. Private offerings of pooled investments (if qualified)

Prohibited Security Types (direct investments of non-pooled securities)

1. Precious metals

2. Venture capital

3. Short sales

4. Covered call options

5. Purchases of letter stock, private placements, or direct payments

6. Mortgages

7. Equipment leasing

8. Leveraged transactions.

9. Commodities transactions.

10. Puts, calls, straddles, or other option strategies used for speculative purposes

11. Direct purchases of real estate, with the exception of REITs

Other Investment Considerations

Bond maturities shall average no more than 10 years. No more than 20% of bonds in the portfolio shall have maturities at any time of greater than 20 years.

Most of the portfolio will be invested in mutual funds. No single mutual fund shall represent more than 30% of the entire value of the portfolio. No individual security held shall represent more than 5% of the total portfolio.

Selection/Retention Criteria for Investments

Investment Management Selection

Investment managers (including mutual funds, money managers and limited partnership sponsors) shall be chosen using the following criteria:

- Past performance, considered relative to other investments having the same investment objective. Consideration shall be given to both performance rankings over various time frames and consistency of performance.

- Costs relative to other funds with like objectives and investment styles.

- The manager's adherence to investment style and size objectives.

- Size of the proposed mutual fund.

- Length of time the fund has been in existence and length of time it has been under the direction of the current manager(s) and whether or not there have been material changes in the manager's organization and personnel.

- The historical volatility and downside risk of each proposed investment.

- How well each proposed investment complements other assets in the portfolio.

- The current economic environment.

Investment Monitoring and Control Procedures

Reports

1. The investment custodian shall provide the Investor with monthly statements for each account that list all assets held by the Investor, values for each asset and all transactions affecting assets within the portfolio, including additions and withdrawals.

2. Advisor shall provide Investor no less frequently than on a quarterly basis, and within 30 days within the end of each such quarter, the following management reports:

   a) Portfolio performance results over the last quarter, year, 3 years and inception-to-date period

   b) Performance results of comparative benchmarks for the last quarter, year, 3 years and 5 years

   c) Performance results of each individual holding for the quarter

   d) Performance shall be reported on a basis that is in compliance with AIMR standards

   e) End-of-quarter status regarding asset allocation—current versus policy

   f) Any recommendations for changes of the above

Meetings and Communication Between Investor and Advisor

As a matter of course, Advisor shall keep Investor apprised of any material changes in the Advisor's outlook, recommended investment policy, and tactics. In addition, Advisor shall meet with Investor approximately annually to review and explain the Portfolio's investment results and any related issues. Advisor shall also be available on a reasonable basis for telephone and email communication as needed.

Any material event that affects the ownership of Advisor's firm or the management of the Portfolio must be reported immediately to Investor.

The Advisor

Wee Manage Money is expected to manage the portfolio in a manner consistent with this Investment Policy Statement and in accordance with state and federal law and the Uniform Prudent Investor Act. Advisor is a registered investment adviser and shall act as the investment advisor and fiduciary to the Investor until the Investor decides otherwise.

Advisor shall be responsible for:

1. Designing, recommending and implementing an appropriate asset allocation plan consistent with the investment objectives, time horizon, risk profile, guidelines and constraints outlined in this statement

2. Recommending an appropriate custodian to safeguard Investor's assets

3. Advising the Investor about the selection of and the allocation of asset categories

4. Identifying specific assets and investment managers within each asset category

5. Ensuring that the custodian provides Investor with a current prospectus, where applicable, for each investment proposed for the portfolio

6. Monitoring the performance of all selected assets

7. Recommending changes to any of the above

8. Periodically reviewing the suitability of the investments for the Investor being available to meet with the Investor at least twice each year, and being available at such other times within reason at the Investor's request

9. Preparing and presenting appropriate reports

Discretion and Title

- Advisor will not take title to any assets. Title shall always be as directed by the Client.

- Investor grants Advisor discretionary control for purchases and sales of securities previously approved by Investor. Advisor shall have no authority to withdraw funds from Investor's accounts, except to cover payment of previously agreed to fees or at Investor's specific written direction.

- Advisor shall be responsible only to make recommendations to the Investor and to implement investment decisions as directed by the Investor.

The Investor

Investor shall be responsible for:

- The oversight of the Portfolio

- Defining the investment objectives and policies of the Portfolio

- Directing Advisor to make changes in investment policy and to oversee and to approve or disapprove Advisor's recommendations with regards to policy, guidelines, objectives and specific investments on a timely basis

- Investor shall provide Advisor with all relevant information on Investor's financial conditions and risk tolerances and shall notify Advisor promptly of any changes to this information

- Investor shall read and understand the information contained in the prospectus and each investment in the Portfolio

- Investor is responsible for exercising all rights, including voting rights, as are acquired through the purchase of securities

Adoption

Adopted by the below signed:

Date:_____

Investor:_____

_____

Advisor:_____

Investment Policy Statement

Keslov Family Trust

Dated: May 15, 1993
IPS dated: December 14, 200X

Big Time Advisors

14 Washington Street
Boise, ID 86868
999/444-6677

Table of Contents

Introduction

The purpose of this Investment Policy Statement (IPS) is to establish a clear understanding between Robert and Jacqueline Keslov, trustees of the Keslov Family Trust ("Investor") and Big Time Advisors ("Advisor") as to the investment goals and objectives and management policies applicable to the Investor's investment portfolio ("Portfolio"). This Investment Policy Statement will:

- Establish reasonable expectations, objectives and guidelines in the investment of the Portfolio's assets

- Create the framework for a well-diversified asset mix that can be expected to generate acceptable long-term returns at a level of risk suitable to the Investor, including:

  — describing an appropriate risk posture for the investment of the Investor's Portfolio

  — specifying the target asset allocation policy

  — establishing investment guidelines regarding the selection of investment managers, permissible securities and diversification of assets

  — specifying the criteria for evaluating the performance of the Portfolio's assets

- Define the responsibilities of the Investor and the Advisor

- Encourage effective communication between the investment manager(s) and the Investor

This IPS is not a contract. This investment policy has not been reviewed by any legal counsel and the Advisor and Investor use it at their own discretion. This IPS is intended to be a summary of an investment philosophy and the procedures that provide guidance for the Investor and the Advisor. The investment policies described in this IPS should be dynamic. These policies should reflect the Investor's current status and philosophy regarding the investment of the Portfolio. These policies will be reviewed and revised periodically to ensure they adequately reflect any changes related to the Portfolio, to the Investor or the capital markets.

It is understood that there can be no guarantee about the attainment of the goals or investment objectives outlined herein.

Investment Policy Discussion

What Is an Investment Policy Statement?

An investment policy outlines and prescribes a prudent and acceptable investment philosophy and defines the investment management procedures and long-term goals for the Investor.

The Uniform Prudent Investor Act ("UPIA") was approved for use in all states at the 1994 annual Conference of Commissioners on Uniform State Law and by the American Bar Association in 1995. The act is applicable to all irrevocable trusts, bypass trusts, QTIPs, ILITs, CRTs, QPRTs, QDTs, and GRTs. Noncompliance with these rules can expose a trustee to significant personal liability. Being clear about the intents, purposes and processes of the trust goes a long way toward protecting the trustee and helping the beneficiaries have clear and appropriate expectations.

Key provisions of the UPIA include:

- No investment is inherently prudent or imprudent, except in how its inclusion or exclusion impacts the portfolio as a whole.

- Trustees are expected to use all reasonably available strategies to improve the risk/reward relationship of the portfolio.

- Under most circumstances, the assets of the trust must be diversified.

- Trustees are obliged to spread portfolio investments across asset classes to enhance performance and reduce risk.

- The possible effect of inflation must be considered as part of the investment strategy. As a result, use of equities is encouraged to allow the possibility that the portfolio's growth will outpace inflation.

- Fiduciaries have a duty to either demonstrate investment skill in managing trust assets or to delegate investment management to another, more qualified party.

Steps to Take to Establish an Investment Policy

1. Assess your financial situation—identify your goals and your needs

2. Determine your tolerance for risk and your time horizon

3. Develop clear objectives for the trust

4. State how the investments are expected to help meet trust objectives

5. Identify any restrictions on the portfolio and its assets

6. Determine the asset classes and mix appropriate (the "Asset Allocation") to maximize the likelihood of achieving the investment objectives at the lowest level of risk

7. Determine the investment methodology to be used with regard to investment (manager) selection, rebalancing, buy-sell disciplines, portfolio reviews and reporting, etc.

8. Implement the decisions

9. Document all investment decisions

The net effort of the written policy is to increase the likelihood that the portfolio will be able to meet the financial needs of the Investor.

Investment Manager Performance Evaluation

Measuring the time-weighted return is not enough; the risk of each investment portfolio should also be considered. A portfolio that slightly underperforms the S&P 500 but carries only half the overall risk is superior on a risk-adjusted basis to a portfolio that slightly outperforms the S&P 500 but carries a full amount of market risk. Deciding when to replace a portfolio manager is often subjective as much as objective. Just because a manager had a down year or two is not a valid reason for replacement. This document lays out the procedures to be followed in order to create a system for making such decisions.

Investor and Account Information

Investor .... Robert and Jacqueline Keslov, Trustees
Keslov Family Trust u/a dated 5/15/1993
5 Younger Court
Boise, ID 86868

Acct. Title	Acct. Number	Approx. Value
Trust .... 5623-4333 .... $1,600,000		

Custodian .... Charles Schwab & Co.

Tax ID Number 76-5678912

Authorized Decision Maker ...... Robert and Jacqueline Keslov, jointly

Investment Advisor .... Big Time Advisors
14 Washington Street
Boise, ID 86868
999/444-6677

Investor Circumstances

The trust beneficiary is Lillian Keslov, 85, who is in fair health. Lillian currently resides in an assisted living facility in Wyoming, which represents her largest monthly expense (approximately $3,500). In addition to the money in the Schwab account, the trust also owns another brokerage account worth approximately $400,000. These funds may eventually be consolidated into the Schwab account. Trust does not require any distributions; principal or income may be withdrawn at the discretion of the trustee.

Upon Lillian's death, the trust will be distributed equally to her two sons, Robert and Willy. Robert has substantial assets already but Willy is of more limited means. Preserving trust principal for eventual distribution to Willy is an important objective.

Investment Objectives

Since the beneficiary does not need much to live on and growth is not required, an investment strategy of Conservative Income is appropriate.

Overall priorities for Investor are, respectively, (1) meeting the current living expenses of the beneficiary, (2) safety of principal, (3) funding a gifting program for family members.

Time Horizon

For the purposes of planning, the time horizon for these investments is to be less than 5 years. Capital values fluctuate over shorter periods and the Investor should recognize that the possibility of capital loss does exist. However, historical asset class return data suggest that the risk of principal loss over a holding period of at least 3 to 5 years can be minimized with the long-term investment mix employed under this Investment Policy Statement.

Tax Policy

The trust is expected to be in a reasonably high marginal federal and state tax bracket for the foreseeable future. Accordingly, tax-efficient mutual funds and tax-free bonds will be considered where applicable.

Risk Tolerance

There are two primary factors that affect the Investor's risk tolerance:

- Financial capacity to accept risk within the investment program
- Willingness to accept return volatility

Personal Financial Capacity

The trust beneficiary is elderly and earns a small income from an annuity. While the trust principal is deemed adequate to meet the future income needs, the Investor does not exhibit financial capacity to take on excess risk.

Willingness to Tolerate Volatility

Given the trustee's desire to preserve principal, there is minimal willingness to tolerate volatility.

Taking these two factors into account, the Investor rates their own risk tolerance as conservative.

Asset Allocation

Academic research suggests that the decision to allocate total assets among various asset classes will far outweigh security selection and other decisions that impact portfolio performance. After reviewing the long-term performance and risk characteristics of various asset classes and balancing the risk and rewards of market behavior, the following asset classes were selected to achieve the objectives of the Investor's Portfolio.

CATEGORY	HOLDINGS	PERCENT	TOTAL
Cash			**10%**
	Money Market Funds	10%	
Bonds			**80%**
	Municipal Bonds	80%	
Stocks			**5%**
	U.S. Large Value Stocks	5%	
Real Estate			**5%**
	REITs	5%	
TOTAL		**100%**	**100%**

No guarantees can be given about future performance, and this Investment Policy Statement shall not be construed as offering such a guarantee.

It should be recognized that the Portfolio may invest in mutual funds; that the actual weightings of these mutual funds can and will vary. As a result, actual returns can be higher or lower than those presented below.

The following discussion is for illustrative purposes, only. Projected returns for a portfolio of assets combined in a manner consistent with the normalized weightings suggested above and using standardized figures for each represented asset class can be estimated. Based on historical norms and adjusted for today's environment suggests that 95% of the time, performance results can be reasonably projected as follows:

Approximated Future Returns For Investor's Allocation Based on Asset Class Categories	ONE YEAR	TEN YEAR
Maximum for Period	15.60%	7.60%
Estimated Average	4.35%	4.35%
Minimum for Period	−5.80%	1.00%

The return calculations above include price appreciation and depreciation, income distributions and capital gains distributions and are **net of estimated income taxes, mutual fund management expenses and advisory fees (pre-tax,** gross returns are estimated at 5.75%). Above figures based on 95% statistical likelihood. Calculations do not include the impact of transaction costs, if any.

Assumptions Used to Calculate Expected Returns		
ASSET CLASS	EXPECTED RETURN (pre-tax)	STANDARD DEVIATION
Cash	4.00%	2.0%
U.S. Large Value Stocks	10.75%	13.0%
Municipal Bonds	5.50%	8.0%
Real Estate	8.25%	14.0%

Updated Allocations

From time to time, it may be desirable to amend the basic allocation policy or calculations. When such changes are made, updates will be attached to this Investment Policy Statement as an Appendix and will be considered part of this Investment Policy Statement.

Rebalancing Procedures

From time to time, market conditions may cause the Portfolio's investment in various asset classes to vary from the established allocation. To remain consistent with the asset allocation guidelines established by this Investment Policy Statement, every quarter the Advisor shall review the portfolio and each asset class in which the Portfolio is invested. If the actual weighting differs from the target weighting by 5% or more from the recommended weighting (e.g., from a recommended 10% to less than 5% or more than 15% of total assets), the Advisor shall rebalance the portfolio back to the recommended weighting. Such rebalancing shall be limited to securities previously approved by Investor.

Frequency of Review

Advisor and Investor should review this Investment Policy Statement together every two years.

Liquidity

The Investor will need to make periodic withdrawals from the portfolio. Therefore, sufficient liquidity shall be maintained among these assets.

Diversification

Investment of the Investor's funds shall be limited to individual marketable securities or packaged products (for example, mutual funds or unit investment trusts) in the following categories:

Permitted Asset Classes

1. Cash and cash equivalents
2. Fixed income–domestic bonds (including investment grade, high yield and municipal bonds)
3. Fixed income–non-U.S. bonds
4. Equities–U.S.
5. Equities–non-U.S.
6. Equities–emerging markets
7. Equities–REITs

Permitted Security Types

1. Mutual funds–stocks, bonds, money market funds
2. Individual stocks
3. Individual bonds, as long as they are rated A or better and traded on a major U.S. exchange
4. Closed-end funds
5. Unit investment trusts
6. Exchange traded funds
7. Deferred annuities issued by an insurance company with a Best rating of A+ or better
8. Bank certificates of deposit

Prohibited Asset Classes and/or Security Types

1. Precious metals

2. Venture capital

3. Short sales

4. Investments in limited partnerships

5. Covered call options

6. Purchases of letter stock, private placements, or direct payments

7. Mortgages

8. Equipment leasing

9. Leveraged transactions

10. Commodities transactions

11. Puts, calls, straddles, or other option strategies, except as permitted above

12. Purchases of real estate, with the exception of REITs

Other Investment Considerations

Bond maturities shall average no more than 10 years. No more than 20% of bonds in the portfolio shall have maturities at any time of greater than 20 years.

Most of the portfolio will be invested in mutual funds and individual municipal bonds. No single mutual fund shall represent more than 30% of the entire value of the portfolio. No individual security held shall represent more than 15% of the total portfolio.

Selection/Retention Criteria for Investments

Investment Management Selection

Investment managers (including mutual funds and money managers) shall be chosen using the following criteria:

- Past performance, considered relative to other investments having the same investment objective. Consideration shall be given to both performance rankings over various time frames and consistency of performance.

- Costs relative to other funds with like objectives and investment styles.

- Size of the proposed mutual fund.

- Length of time the fund has been in existence and length of time it has been under the direction of the current manager(s) and whether or not there have been material changes in the manager's organization and personnel.

- The historical volatility and downside risk of each proposed investment.

- How well each proposed investment complements other assets in the portfolio.

- The current economic environment.

- The likelihood of future investment success, relative to other opportunities.

FAMILY TRUST

Investment Monitoring and Control Procedures

Reports

1. Charles Schwab & Co. shall provide Investor with a report each month that lists all assets held by Investor, values for each asset and all transactions affecting assets within the portfolio, including additions and withdrawals.

2. Investor shall receive no less frequently than on a quarterly basis, and within 30 days within the end of each such quarter, the following management reports:

   a) Portfolio performance results over the last quarter, year, 3 years and inception-to-date period

   b) Performance results of each individual manager for the same periods

   c) Performance results of comparative benchmarks for the same periods

   d) Performance shall be reported on a basis that is in compliance with AIMR standards

   e) End-of-quarter status regarding asset allocation—current versus policy

   f) Any recommendations for changes of the above

Meetings and Communication Between Investor and Advisor

As a matter of course, Big Time Advisors shall keep Investor apprised of any material changes in Big Time Advisors's outlook, recommended investment policy, and tactics. In addition, Big Time Advisors shall meet with Investor approximately annually to review and explain the Portfolio's investment results and any related issues. Big Time Advisors shall also be available on a reasonable basis for telephone and e-mail communication as needed.

Any material event that affects the ownership of Big Time Advisors' firm or the management of the Portfolio must be reported immediately to Investor.

Duties and Responsibilities

The Advisor

Big Time Advisors is expected to manage the Portfolio in a manner consistent with this Investment Policy Statement and in accordance with state and federal law and the Uniform Prudent Investor Act. Big Time Advisors is a registered investment adviser and shall act as the investment advisor and fiduciary to the Investor until the Investor decides otherwise.

Big Time Advisors shall be responsible for:

1. Designing, recommending and implementing an appropriate asset allocation plan consistent with the investment objectives, time horizon, risk profile, guidelines and constraints outlined in this statement

2. Recommending an appropriate custodian to safeguard Investor's assets

3. Advising the Investor about the selection of and the allocation of asset categories

4. Identifying specific assets and investment managers within each asset category

5. Ensuring that the custodian provides Investor with a current prospectus, where applicable, for each investment proposed for the portfolio

6. Monitoring the performance of all selected assets

7. Recommending changes to any of the above

8. Periodically reviewing the suitability of the investments for the Investor

9. Being available to meet with the Investor at least twice each year, and being available at such other times within reason at the Investor's request

10. Preparing and presenting appropriate reports

Discretion and Title

Big Time Advisors will not take title to any assets.

Investor grants Big Time Advisors discretionary control (for purchases and sales only) over the Investor's assets which are held in the accounts to be managed by Big Time Advisors under this Investment Policy Statement. Advisor shall have no authority to withdraw funds from Investor's accounts, except to cover payment of previously agreed to fees or at Investor's specific direction.

The Investor

Investor shall be responsible for:

1. The oversight of the Portfolio

2. Defining the investment objectives and policies of the Portfolio

3. Directing Big Time Advisors to make changes in investment policy and to oversee and to approve or disapprove Big Time Advisors's recommendations with regards to policy, guidelines, objectives and specific investments on a timely basis

4. Investor shall provide Big Time Advisors with all relevant information on Investor's financial conditions and risk tolerances and shall notify Big Time Advisors promptly of any changes to this information

5. Investor shall read and understand the information contained in the prospectus and each investment in the Portfolio

Adoption

Adopted by the below signed:

Date:_____

Investor:_____

_____

Advisor:_____

IPS Statement for a Charitable Remainder Trust

Investment Policy Statement

The Robert Jones CRT

December 14, 200X

Balanced Financial Advisors

600 California Avenue
San Francisco, CA 94104
415/999-8888

Table of Contents

Introduction

The purpose of this Investment Policy Statement (IPS) is to establish a clear understanding between Robert Jones, trustee for the Robert Jones CRT ("Investor") and Balanced Financial Advisors ("Advisor") as to the investment goals and objectives and management policies applicable to the Investor's investment portfolio ("Portfolio"). This Investment Policy Statement:

- Establishes the Investor's expectations, objectives and guidelines in the investment of the Portfolio's assets
- Creates the framework for a well-diversified asset mix that can be expected to generate acceptable long-term returns at a level of risk suitable to the Investor, including:
  - describing an appropriate risk posture for the investment of the Investor's Portfolio
  - specifying the target asset allocation policy
  - establishing investment guidelines regarding the selection of investment managers, permissible securities and diversification of assets
  - specifying the criteria for evaluating the performance of the Portfolio's assets
- Defines the responsibilities of the Investor and the Advisor
- Encourages effective communication between the investment manager(s) and the Investor

This IPS is not a contract. This investment policy has not been reviewed by any legal counsel and the Advisor and Investor use it at their own discretion. This IPS is intended to be a summary of an investment philosophy and the procedures that provide guidance for the Investor and the Advisor. The investment policies described in this IPS should be dynamic. These policies should reflect the Investor's current status and philosophy regarding the investment of the Portfolio.

These policies will be reviewed and revised periodically to ensure they adequately reflect any changes related to the Portfolio, to the Investor or the capital markets.

It is understood that there can be no guarantee about the attainment of the goals or investment objectives outlined herein.

Investment Policy Discussion

What Is an Investment Policy Statement?

An investment policy outlines and prescribes a prudent and acceptable investment philosophy and defines the investment management procedures and long-term goals for the Investor.

The Need for a Written Policy

The principal reason for developing a long-term investment policy and for putting it in writing is to enable you and us to protect your portfolio from ad hoc revisions of sound long-term policy. Without an investment policy, in times of market turmoil, investors may be inclined to make ad hoc investment decisions that are inconsistent with prudent investment management principles. Your investment policy provides a well-thought-out framework from which sound investment decisions can be made.

The development of an investment policy follows the basic approach underlying financial planning: assessing your financial condition, setting goals, developing a strategy to meet the goals, implementing the strategy, regularly reviewing the results and adjusting the strategy or the implementation as circumstances dictate. In following an investment policy, you'll employ a more disciplined and systematic approach and thereby increase the probability of satisfying your investment goals.

The Uniform Prudent Investor Act ("UPIA") was approved for use in all states at the 1994 annual Conference of Commissioners on Uniform State Law and by the American Bar Association in 1995. The act is applicable to all irrevocable trusts, bypass trusts, QTIPs, ILITs, CRTs, QPRTs, QDTs, and GRTs.

Noncompliance with these rules can expose a trustee to significant personal liability.

Being clear about the intents, purposes and processes of the trust goes a long way toward protecting the trustee and helping the beneficiaries have clear and appropriate expectations.

Key provisions of the UPIA include:

- No investment is inherently prudent or imprudent, except in how its inclusion or exclusion affects the portfolio as a whole.

- Trustees are expected to use all reasonably available strategies to improve the risk/reward relationship of the portfolio.

- Under most circumstances, the assets of the trust must be diversified.

- Trustees are obliged to spread portfolio investments across asset classes to enhance performance and reduce risk.

- The possible effect of inflation must be considered as part of the investment strategy.

- As a result, use of equities is encouraged to allow the possibility that the portfolio's growth will outpace inflation.

- Fiduciaries have a duty to either demonstrate investment skill in managing trust assets or to delegate investment management to another, more qualified party.

Steps to Take to Establish an Investment Policy

1. Assess your financial situation—identify your goals and your needs

2. Determine your tolerance for risk and your time horizon

3. Develop clear objectives for the trust

4. State how the investments are expected to help meet trust objectives

5. Identify any restrictions on the portfolio and its assets

6. Determine the asset classes and mix appropriate (the "Asset Allocation") to maximize the likelihood of achieving the investment objectives at the lowest level of risk

7. Determine the investment methodology to be used with regard to investment (manager) selection, rebalancing, buy-sell disciplines, portfolio reviews and reporting, etc.

8. Implement the decisions

9. Document all investment decisions

The net effort of the written policy is to increase the likelihood that the portfolio will be able to meet the financial needs of the Investor.

Overview Commentary and Information

Investor Information

Trustee . . . . .Robert Jones

Trust Data . . . . .The Robert Jones CRT, dated 2/29/2000

Trust Federal Tax Identification Number 94-3328465

Client . . . . .Robert Jones, Trustee
The Robert Jones CRT
550 Florida Place
Walnut Creek, CA 90000

Account Information

Acct. Title	Acct. Number	Approx. Value
The Robert Jones CRT	12345678	$1,073,589

Custodian . . . . .Charles Schwab & Co.

Tax ID Number 94-3327744

Authorized Decision Maker . . . . .Robert Jones, Trustee

Investment Advisor .Balanced Financial Advisors
600 California Avenue
San Francisco, CA 94104
415/999-8888

Tax Preparation . . . . .Greg Accountant
Big CPA Firm

Investor Circumstances

This charitable remainder trust is set up to benefit Robert Jones, the grantor and trustee, through his lifetime. Since Robert is in his late 30s, the trust should be invested to last a very long time. The payout on the trust has been set at 5%. Because the goal is to have assets remaining for the benefit of charity, prudent investor rules will be applied.

The administration of the trust provides for a unitrust payment of five percent (5%) of the net fair market value of the trust assets valued as of the first day of each taxable year of the trust.

Investment Philosophy

The basic tenets under which this portfolio will be managed include the following:

1. Modern portfolio theory, as recognized by the 1990 Nobel Prize, will be the philosophical foundation for how the portfolio will be

structured and how subsequent decisions will be made. The under-lying concepts of modern portfolio theory include:

- Investors are risk averse. The only acceptable risk is that which is adequately compensated by potential portfolio returns.

- Markets are efficient. It is virtually impossible to anticipate the future direction of the market as a whole or of any individual security. It is, therefore, unlikely that any portfolio will succeed in consistently "beating the market."

- The design of the portfolio as a whole is more important than the selection of any particular security within the portfolio. The appropriate allocation of capital among asset classes (stocks, bonds, cash, etc.) will have far more influence on long-term portfolio results than the selection of individual securities. Investing for the long term (preferably longer than ten years) becomes critical to investment success because it allows the long-term characteristics of the asset classes to surface.

- For a given risk level, an optimal combination of asset classes will maximize returns. Diversification helps reduce investment volatility. The proportional mix of asset classes determines the long-term risk and return characteristics of the portfolio as a whole.

- Portfolio risk can be decreased by increasing diversification of the portfolio and by lowering the correlation of market behavior among the asset classes selected. (Correlation is the statistical term for the extent to which two asset classes move in tandem or opposition to one another.)

2. Investing globally helps to minimize overall portfolio risk due to the imperfect correlation between economies of the world. Investing globally has also been shown historically to enhance portfolio returns, although there is no guarantee that it will do so in the future.

3. Equities offer the potential for higher long-term investment returns than cash or fixed income investments. Equities are also more volatile in their performance. Investors seeking higher rates of

return must increase the proportion of equities in their portfolio, while at the same time accepting greater variation of results (including occasional declines in value).

Given these tenets, the underlying approach to managing this Portfolio shall be to optimize the risk/return relationship appropriate to Investor's needs and goals. The Portfolio will be diversified globally, employing a variety of asset classes. Mutual funds or managed portfolios will be employed to implement the Portfolio and the chosen asset classes will be periodically rebalanced to maintain a more consistent risk/reward profile.

Investment Objectives

The overall priorities for Investor are, respectively, (1) providing increasing lifetime income and (2) Providing for a charitable remainder.

The long-term objective for the assets under this policy is to achieve a pre-tax average annual return of 4.8% above inflation over the holding period of this portfolio.

Time Horizon

For the purposes of planning, the time horizon for the investments in this Portfolio will parallel the lifetime of the Investor. It is assumed that the investment horizon for this Portfolio greatly exceeds ten (10) years.

Withdrawals from this Portfolio are being made on a quarterly basis.

Capital values do fluctuate over shorter periods and the Investor should recognize that the possibility of capital loss does exist. However, historical asset-class return data suggest that the risk of principal loss over a holding period of at least three to five years can be minimized with the long-term investment mix employed under this Investment Policy Statement.

Tax Policy

Taxation is for the most part not a consideration in this Portfolio, although normal four-tier accounting will apply to the trust assets.

Risk Tolerance

There are two primary factors that affect the Investor's risk tolerance:

- Financial capacity to accept risk within the investment program
- Willingness to accept return volatility

Personal Financial Capacity

Given other assets, Investor has considerable financial capacity to take on risk. This needs to be balanced with the goal of maintaining a benefit for the remainderman.

Willingness to Tolerate Volatility

The Investor desires long-term investment growth sufficient to meet their objectives and the objectives of the trust. The Investor understands that to achieve such growth, the Portfolio will experience periods of decline. He further understands that in a severe market, the potential recovery period could exceed three years.

Although Investor prefers to limit the Portfolio's volatility, there is a willingness to accept occasional moderate declines in order to position the Portfolio for improved growth possibilities.

Taking these two factors into account, the Investor's risk tolerance may be characterized as moderate.

Asset Allocation

Academic research offers considerable evidence that the asset allocation decision far outweighs security selection and market timing in its impact on portfolio performance. After reviewing the long-term performance and risk characteristics of various asset classes and balancing the risk and rewards of market behavior, the following asset classes were selected to achieve the objectives of the Investor's Portfolio.

ASSET ALLOCATION

CATEGORY	HOLDINGS	RANGE	TOTAL
Cash		**1–5%**	**1%**
	Money Market Funds	1–5%	
Bonds		**19–45%**	**29%**
	Corporate Bonds	16%	
Stocks		**50–75%**	**66%**
	U.S. Large Stocks	20–40%	
	U.S. Small Socks	7–15%	
	International Stocks	15–25%	
	Emerging Mkt Stocks	2–10%	
Real Estate		**2–10%**	**4%**
	REITs	2–10%	
TOTAL		**100%**	**100%**

Note: Within the above allocation, the following broad limits will apply:

- Bonds and cash to never exceed 50% nor to fall below 20% in aggregate

- Stocks, including REITs, to never exceed 80% nor to fall below 50%.

The Normal Allocation:

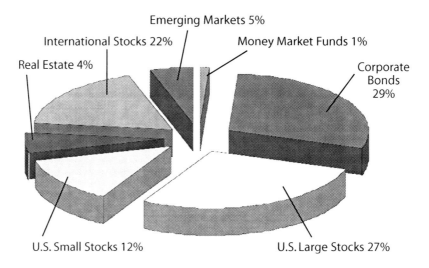

Historical Portfolio Returns & Volatility

The following historical returns reflect the results of this portfolio, as normally constructed, over the 1972 to 200X time period.

Bear in mind, these outcomes represent historical results using index data and estimated expenses. It should be recognized that the portfolio will invest in mutual funds or other securities and that the actual weighting of these securities can and will vary. It is also important to note that the future returns of the securities with the portfolio can be expected to vary from the historical returns referenced.

The portfolio results referenced reflect a portfolio design having a "value" orientation (i.e., employing funds or stocks with below-average price-to-book ratios). Historically, over-weighting "value" investments in a portfolio has resulted in higher portfolio returns with lower risk when compared to portfolios with greater "growth" characteristics. The Investor's Portfolio will be designed with a "value" orientation.

The Portfolio's historical rate of return is not a guarantee of future investment returns. Future returns could differ significantly and capital loss is possible. This Investment Policy Statement shall not be construed as offering a guarantee.

Historical Portfolio & Asset Class Returns (1972 to 200X)		
ASSET CLASS	**HISTORICAL RETURN**	**STANDARD DEVIATION**
Deviation Portfolio Return (geometric mean)	11.8%	11.4%
Less Estimated Expenses	1.7%	
Portfolio Return (net)	10.1%	
Less Inflation (5.0% + 0.3% compounding)	5.3%	1.2%
Real Return After Inflation	4.8%	
Asset Class Returns (before expenses):		
Cash	6.6%	0.8%
Intermediate Bonds	8.5%	4.9%
U.S. Large Stocks	12.2%	17.5%
U.S. Small Stocks	13.3%	24.8%
International Stocks	11.2%	19.1%
Emerging Market Stocks*	11.3%	27.8%
Real Estate	12.5%	15.4%

* Emerging Market data since 1988

Historical Rolling Period Real Returns (1972 to 200X)		
	ROLLING ONE-YEAR PERIODS	**ROLLING FIVE-YEAR PERIODS**
Annualized Returns:		
Best Periods	42.0%	21.0%
Average (arithmetic mean)	5.4%	6.3%
Worst Period	−35.2%	−4.4%
% of Periods generating:		
Negative Returns	27.2%	9.3%
Less than CPI + 4%	47.3%	30.9%

Updated Allocations

The allocation, as identified above, allows for a range of allocations within each asset class. Advisor shall retain and Investor grants Advisor the right to make changes within the range(s) specified as Advisor determines appropriate based on Advisor's sole insight with regard to the economy, the markets and the general investing environment. Changes shall be made by Advisor with the intent of enhancing the likelihood of the portfolio attaining the objectives as stated above.

At all times a target asset allocation shall exist and Investor shall be so notified by Advisor of changes to target.

Over time, it may be desirable to amend the basic allocation policy or calculations. When such changes are made, updates will be attached to this Investment Policy Statement as an Appendix and will be considered part of this Investment Policy Statement.

Rebalancing Procedures

From time to time, market conditions may cause the Portfolio's investment in various asset classes to vary from the established allocation. To remain consistent with the asset allocation guidelines established by this Investment Policy Statement and as established in writing by Advisor, every quarter the Advisor shall review the portfolio and each asset class in which the Portfolio is invested. If the actual weighting differs from the target weighting by 5% or more from the recommended weighting (e.g., from a recommended 10% to less than 5% or more than 15% of total assets), the Advisor shall rebalance the portfolio back to the recommended weighting. Such rebalancing shall be limited to securities previously approved by Investor.

Frequency of Review

The Investor recognizes that all investments go through cycles and, therefore, there will be periods of time in which the investment objectives are not met or when specific managers fail to meet their expected performance expectations.

The Investor accepts the principle that, in the absence of specific circumstances requiring immediate action, patience and a longer-term perspective will be employed when evaluating investment performance.

On an overall portfolio basis, the Investor establishes a goal of evaluating portfolio investment performance relative to investment benchmarks over a minimum time period of five years.

Advisor and Investor should review this Investment Policy Statement together every two years.

Liquidity

Since distributions are being made on a quarterly basis, all dividends and capital gains will be maintained in cash reserves rather than be reinvested.

Diversification

Investment of the Investor's funds shall be limited to individual marketable securities or packaged products (for example, mutual funds or unit investment trusts) in the following categories:

Permitted Asset Classes

1. Cash and cash equivalents
2. Fixed income–domestic bonds (including investment grade, high yield and municipal bonds)

3. Fixed income–non-U.S. bonds

4. Equities–U.S.

5. Equities–non-U.S.

6. Equities–emerging markets

7. Equities–REITs

8. Alternative investments

Permitted Security Types

1. Mutual funds–stocks, bonds, money market funds

2. Individual stocks

3. Individual bonds, as long as they are rated A or better and traded on a major U.S. exchange

4. Closed-end funds

5. Unit investment trusts

6. Exchange traded funds

7. Private offerings of pooled investments (if qualified)

Prohibited Security Types

1. Precious metals

2. Venture capital

3. Short sales

4. Covered call options

5. Purchases of letter stock, private placements, or direct payments

6. Mortgages

7. Equipment leasing

8. Leveraged transactions

9. Commodities transactions

10. Puts, calls, straddles, or other option strategies used for speculative purposes

11. Direct purchases of real estate, with the exception of REITs

Other Investment Considerations

Bond maturities shall average no more than 10 years. No more than 20% of bonds in the Portfolio shall have maturities at any time of greater than 20 years.

Most of the Portfolio will be invested in mutual funds. No single mutual fund shall represent more than 30% of the entire value of the Portfolio.

No individual security held shall represent more than 5% of the total Portfolio.

Selection/Retention Criteria for Investments

Investment Management Selection

Investment managers (including mutual funds, money managers and limited partnership sponsors) shall be chosen using the following criteria:

- Past performance, considered relative to other investments having the same investment objective. Consideration shall be given to both performance rankings over various time frames and consistency of performance.

- Costs relative to other funds with like objectives and investment styles.

- The manager's adherence to investment style and size objectives.

- Size of the proposed mutual fund.

- Length of time the fund has been in existence and length of time it has been under the direction of the current manager(s) and whether or not there have been material changes in the manager's organization and personnel.

- The historical volatility and downside risk of each proposed investment.

- How well each proposed investment complements other assets in the Portfolio.

- The current economic environment.

Investment Monitoring and Control Procedures

Reports

1. The investment custodian shall provide Investor with monthly statements for each account that list all assets held by Investor, values for each asset and all transactions affecting assets within the Portfolio, including additions and withdrawals.

2. Balanced Financial Advisors shall provide Investor no less frequently than on a quarterly basis and within 30 days within the end of each such quarter the following management reports:

   a) Portfolio performance results over the last quarter, year, 3 years and inception-to-date period

   b) Performance results of comparative benchmarks for the last quarter, year, 3 years and 5 years

   c) Performance results of each individual holding for the quarter

   d) Performance shall be reported on a basis that is in compliance with AIMR standards

   e) End of quarter status regarding asset allocation—current versus policy

   f) Any recommendations for changes of the above

Meetings and Communication Between Investor and Advisor

As a matter of course, Balanced Financial Advisors shall keep Investor apprised of any material changes in Balanced Financial Advisors' outlook, recommended investment policy, and tactics. In addition, Balanced Financial Advisors shall meet with Investor approximately annually to review and explain the Portfolio's investment results and any related issues. Balanced Financial Advisors shall also be available on a reasonable basis for telephone and e-mail communication as needed.

Any material event that affects the ownership of Balanced Financial Advisors' firm or the management of the Portfolio must be reported immediately to Investor.

Duties and Responsibilities

The Advisor

Balanced Financial Advisors is expected to manage the Portfolio in a manner consistent with this Investment Policy Statement and in accordance with State and Federal law and the Uniform Prudent Investor Act. Balanced Financial Advisors is a registered investment adviser and shall act as the investment advisor and fiduciary to the Investor until the Investor decides otherwise.

Balanced Financial Advisors shall be responsible for:

1. Designing, recommending and implementing an appropriate asset allocation plan consistent with the investment objectives, time horizon, risk profile, guidelines and constraints outlined in this statement

2. Recommending an appropriate custodian to safeguard Investor's assets

3. Advising the Investor about the selection of and the allocation of asset categories

4. Identifying specific assets and investment managers within each asset category

5. Ensuring that the custodian provides Investor with a current prospectus, where applicable, for each investment proposed for the portfolio

6. Monitoring the performance of all selected assets

7. Recommending changes to any of the above

8. Periodically reviewing the suitability of the investments for the Investor

9. Being available to meet with the Investor at least once each year, and being available at such other times within reason at the Investor's request

10. Preparing and presenting appropriate reports

Discretion and Title

- Balanced Financial Advisors will not take title to any assets.

- Balanced Financial Advisors shall be responsible only to make recommendations to the Investor and to implement investment decisions as directed by the Investor.

The Investor

Investor shall be responsible for:

1. The oversight of the Portfolio

2. Defining the investment objectives and policies of the Portfolio

3. Directing Balanced Financial Advisors to make changes in investment policy and to oversee and to approve or disapprove Balanced Financial Advisors' recommendations with regard to policy, guidelines, objectives and specific investments on a timely basis

4. Providing Balanced Financial Advisors with all relevant information on Investor's financial conditions and risk tolerances and notifying Balanced Financial Advisors promptly of any changes to this information.

5. Reading and understanding the information contained in the prospectus and each investment in the Portfolio.

6. Exercising all rights, including voting rights, as are acquired through the purchase of securities.

Adoption

Adopted by the below signed:

Date:_____

Investor:_____

_____

Advisor:_____

Investment Policy Statement

XYZ College Endowment Fund

August 31, 200X

Charitable Advisors, Inc.

College Station, KS

Table of Contents

Introduction

The purpose of this Investment Policy Statement (IPS) is to establish a clear understanding between XYZ College Endowment Fund Trustees ("Investor") and Charitable Advisors, Inc. ("Advisor") as to the investment goals and objectives and management policies applicable to the Investor's investment portfolio ("Portfolio"). This Investment Policy Statement will:

- Establish reasonable expectations, objectives and guidelines in the investment of the Portfolio's assets

- Create the framework for a well-diversified asset mix that can be expected to generate acceptable long-term returns at a level of risk suitable to the Investor, including:

  — describing an appropriate risk posture for the investment of the Investor's Portfolio

  — specifying the target asset allocation policy

  — establishing investment guidelines regarding the selection of investment managers, permissible securities and diversification of assets

  — specifying the criteria for evaluating the performance of the Portfolio's assets

- Define the responsibilities of the Investor and the Advisor

- Encourage effective communication between the investment manager(s) and the Investor

This IPS is not a contract. This investment policy has not been reviewed by any legal counsel and the Advisor and Investor use it at their own discretion. This IPS is intended to be a summary of an investment philosophy and the procedures that provide guidance for the Investor and the Advisor. The investment policies described in this IPS should be dynamic. These policies should reflect the Investor's current status and philosophy regarding the investment of the Portfolio. These policies will be reviewed and revised periodically to ensure they adequately reflect any changes related to the Portfolio, to the Investor or the capital markets.

It is understood that there can be no guarantee about the attainment of the goals or investment objectives outlined herein.

Investment Policy Discussion

What Is an Investment Policy Statement?

An investment policy outlines and prescribes a prudent and acceptable investment philosophy and defines the investment management procedures and long-term goals for the Investor.

The Uniform Prudent Investor Act ("UPIA") was approved for use in all states at the 1994 annual Conference of Commissioners on Uniform State Law and by the American Bar Association in 1995. The act provides excellent guidance about the "prudent investment process."

Key provisions of the UPIA include:

- No investment is inherently prudent or imprudent, except in how its inclusion or exclusion impacts the portfolio as a whole.

- Trustees are expected to use all reasonably available strategies to improve the risk/reward relationship of the portfolio.

- Under most circumstances, the assets of the trust must be diversified.

- Trustees are obliged to spread portfolio investments across asset classes to enhance performance and reduce risk.

- The possible effect of inflation must be considered as part of the investment strategy. As a result, use of equities is encouraged to allow the possibility that the portfolio's growth will outpace inflation.

- Fiduciaries have a duty to either demonstrate investment skill in managing trust assets or to delegate investment management to another, more qualified party.

Steps to Take to Establish an Investment Policy

1. Assess your financial situation—identify your goals and your needs

2. Determine your tolerance for risk and your time horizon

3. Develop clear objectives for the endowment

4. State how the investments are expected to help meet trust objectives

5. Identify any restrictions on the portfolio and its assets

6. Determine the asset classes and mix appropriate (the "Asset Allocation") to maximize the likelihood of achieving the investment objectives at the lowest level of risk

7. Determine the investment methodology to be used with regard to investment (manager) selection, rebalancing, buy-sell disciplines, portfolio reviews and reporting, etc.

8. Implement the decisions

9. Document all investment decisions

The net effort of the written policy is to increase the likelihood that the portfolio will be able to meet the financial needs of the Investor.

Investment Manager Performance Evaluation

Measuring the time-weighted return is not enough; the risk of each investment portfolio should also be considered. A portfolio that slightly underperforms the S&P 500 but carries only half the overall risk is superior on a risk-adjusted basis to a portfolio that slightly outperforms the S&P 500 but carries a full amount of market risk. Deciding when to replace a portfolio manager is often subjective as much as objective. Just because a manager had a down year or two is not a valid reason for replacement. This document lays out the procedures to be followed in order to create a system for making such decisions.

It is understood that there can be no guarantee about the attainment of the goals or investment objectives outlined herein.

Overview Commentary

The XYZ College Endowment Fund was created in 1957 as a result of a $1 million gift from Ebenezer Scrooge. It is operated for the benefit of the university and its communities of interest, as determined by the Endowment Trustees. It is valued today at $125 million and provides approximately $6.2 million each year for student financial aid and building upgrades for the campus.

Client and Account Information

Primary Contact . . . . Jeremiah Johnson

Investment Account

Custodian . . . . Bank of New York

Account Number 2345-67891

Tax ID Number 84-1234567

Authorized Decision Maker . . . . The Endowment Trustees

Account Value . . . . Approximately $125 million

Investment Advisor . . . . Charitable Advisors, Inc.
College Station, KS

Key Contacts for Plan

The Trustees . . . . Sarah McKee, University President
Jeremiah Johnson, University CFO
John Smith, Chairman of Endowment Trustees

Economic Outlook

The Endowment Trustees primarily rely on the insight of the XYZ College Economics Department, as presented by the department chair Dr. Mary Optimist. The insights gained and relied upon for investment decisions for the endowment include:

- Long-term U.S. economic growth of 3.5%

- Long-term growth of the EAFE countries—4.2%

- Interest rates staying steady at approximately their current rates

- Inflation in the U.S. averaging approximately 2.5% over the next ten years

XYZ College is working hard to become an accredited institution. Their next audit by the accrediting authorities will be in about two years and they are hopeful to be awarded full accreditation at that time. If so, they expect enrollment to rise from its current level of 800 to at least twice that.

The endowment itself has been increasing over the years as the revenues from the oil platforms off the Louisiana coast, which were given to the endowment as a gift from a former student who could not find any other way to get rid of the investment, have been rising. In fact, income from the oil has generated roughly $15 million each of the last several years and that is expected to continue for the foreseeable future.

Annual distributions from the endowment are set at 5% of the endowment value as of the prior calendar year-end. Since distributions have been substantially below the oil income, the endowment has been rising significantly.

The basic tenets under which this portfolio will be managed include the following:

1. Modern portfolio theory, as recognized by the 1990 Nobel Prize, will be the primary influence driving the way the portfolio will be structured and how subsequent decisions will be made. The underlying concepts of modern portfolio theory include:

   - Investors are risk averse. The only acceptable risk is that which is adequately compensated by potential portfolio returns.

   - Markets are efficient. It is virtually impossible to know ahead of time the next direction of the market as a whole or of any individual security. It is, therefore, unlikely that any portfolio will succeed in consistently "beating the market."

   - The portfolio as a whole is more important than an individual security. The appropriate allocation of capital among asset classes (stocks, bonds, cash, etc.) will have far more influence on long-term portfolio results than the selection of individual securities. Investing for the long term (preferably longer than ten years) becomes critical to investment success because it allows the long-term characteristics of the asset classes to surface.

   - For every risk level, there exists an optimal combination of asset classes that will maximize returns. A diverse set of asset classes will be selected to help minimize risk. The proportionality of the mix of asset classes will determine the long-term risk and return characteristics of the portfolio as a whole.

   - Portfolio risk can be decreased by increasing diversification of the portfolio and by lowering the correlation of market behavior among the asset classes selected. (Correlation is the statistical term for the extent to which two asset classes move in tandem or opposition to one another.)

2. Investing globally helps to minimize overall portfolio risk due to the imperfect correlation between economies of the world. Investing

globally has also been shown historically to enhance portfolio returns, although there is no guarantee that it will do so in the future.

3. Equities offer the potential for higher long-term investment returns than cash or fixed income investments. Equities are also more volatile in their performance. Investors seeking higher rates of return must increase the proportion of equities in their portfolio, while at the same time accepting greater variation of results (including occasional declines in value).

4. Picking individual securities and timing the purchase or sale of investments in the attempt to "beat the market" are highly unlikely to increase long-term investment returns; they also can significantly increase portfolio operating costs. Such practices are, therefore, to be avoided.

5. The basic underlying approach to the management of this portfolio shall therefore be to optimize the risk-return relationship appropriate to Investor's needs and goals using a globally diverse portfolio of a variety of asset classes using mutual funds or managed portfolios, to "buy and hold" the selected securities and periodically re-optimize (rebalance).

Investment Objectives

The specific objectives for these assets shall be to achieve an average annual rate of return (over a period of five years) of the Consumer Price Index plus 4% for the aggregate investments under this Investment Policy Statement.

Time Horizon

For the purposes of planning, the time horizon for these investments is to be in excess of 10 years. The trustees hope and expect that the endowment will last effectively forever, supporting the school and its mission for as long as it can.

Capital values do fluctuate over shorter periods and the trustees recognize that the possibility of capital loss does exist. However, historical asset class return data suggest that the risk of principal loss over a holding period of at least three to five years can be minimized with the long-term investment mix employed under this Investment Policy Statement.

Risk Tolerance

Investment theory and historical capital market return data suggest that, over long periods of time, there is a relationship between the level or risk assumed and the level of return that can be expected in an investment program. In general, higher risk (e.g., volatility of return) is associated with higher return.

Given this relationship between risk and return, a fundamental step in determining the investment policy for the Portfolio is the determination of an appropriate risk tolerance. There are two primary factors that affect the Investor's risk tolerance:

- Financial ability to accept risk within the investment program
- Willingness to accept return volatility

Taking these two factors into account, the Investor rates his or her own risk tolerance as moderate. The Investor recognizes that higher returns involve some volatility and has indicated a willingness to tolerate declines in the value of this portfolio of between 0% and 10% in a given year. The Investor would accept declines in value as often as two out of ten years to achieve higher returns.

Asset Allocation

Academic research suggests that the decision to allocate total assets among various asset classes will far outweigh security selection and other decisions that affect portfolio performance. After reviewing the long-term performance and risk characteristics of various asset classes and balancing the risk and rewards of market behavior, the following asset classes were selected to achieve the objectives of the Investor's Portfolio.

ASSET ALLOCATION			
CATEGORY	HOLDINGS	PERCENT	TOTAL
Cash			4%
	U.S. Treasury Bills	3%	
	Taxable Money Market Funds	1%	
Bonds			36%
	Short-Term Gov't.	5%	
	Intermediate-Term Gov't.	5%	
	High Grade Corporates	15%	
	High Yield Bonds	4%	
	Convertible Bonds	7%	
Stocks			50%
	Large Cap Growth Stocks	12%	
	Large Cap Value Stocks	14%	
	Small Cap Growth Stocks	4%	
	Small Cap Value Stocks	5%	
	International Stocks	12%	
	Emerging Market Stocks	3%	
Real Estate			10%
	Direct Real Estate Investments	8%	
	REITs	2%	
TOTAL		100%	100%

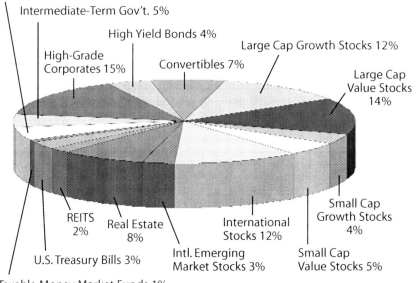

Short-Term Gov't. 5%

Intermediate-Term Gov't. 5%

High Yield Bonds 4%

High-Grade Corporates 15%

Convertibles 7%

Large Cap Growth Stocks 12%

Large Cap Value Stocks 14%

REITS 2%

Real Estate 8%

International Stocks 12%

Small Cap Growth Stocks 4%

U.S. Treasury Bills 3%

Intl. Emerging Market Stocks 3%

Small Cap Value Stocks 5%

Taxable Money Market Funds 1%

No guarantees can be given about future performance, and this Investment Policy Statement shall not be construed as offering such a guarantee.

It should be recognized that some of the Portfolio will be invested in mutual funds, and that the actual weightings of these mutual funds can and will vary. As a result, actual returns can be higher or lower than those presented below.

Solely for illustrative purposes, a portfolio of assets (exclusive of any funds which may be managed elsewhere) combined in a manner consistent with the normalized weightings suggested above and using standardized figures for each represented asset class based on historical norms and adjusted for today's environment suggests that 95% of the time, performance results can be reasonably projected as follows:

Approximated Future Returns
For Investor's Allocation Based on Asset Class Categories

	ONE YEAR	TEN YEAR
Maximum for Period	28.2%	16.4%
Estimated Average	8.9%	8.9%
Minimum for Period	−12.3%	2.6%
Worst-Case Conditions	−21.3%	−0.5%

All return calculations herein include price appreciation/depreciation, income distributions and capital gains distributions. Above figures based on 95% statistical likelihood, except for those of "Worst-Case Conditions," which returns are expected to exceed all but 5% of the time. Calculations do not include the impact of management fees, transaction costs or taxes.

On average, over long periods of time, this portfolio design can be expected to experience losses two in eight years, and in such cases should take an average of somewhat less than ten months to recover such losses. Over a five-year period, such a portfolio's performance should exceed inflation 72% of the time.

Assumptions Used to Calculate Expected Returns

ASSET CLASS	EXPECTED RETURN (pre-tax)	STANDARD DEVIATION
Cash & Equivalents	3.2%	1.9%
Intermediate Govt Bonds	5.2%	6.1%
High Yield Bonds	8.6%	9.2%
Large Cap U.S. Stocks	11.3%	14.1%
Small Cap U.S. Stocks	12.4%	18.1%
Foreign Stocks	10.7%	15.1%
Emerging Mkt Stocks	13.2%	21.4%
REITs	10.8%	9.1%

Note: All these figures are imaginary. Do not use them as a resource.

Updated Allocations

From time to time, it may be desirable to amend the basic allocation policy or calculations. When such changes are made, updates will be attached to this Investment Policy Statement as an Appendix and will be considered part of this Investment Policy Statement.

Rebalancing Procedures

From time to time, market conditions may cause the Portfolio's investment in various asset classes to vary from the established allocation. To remain consistent with the asset allocation guidelines established by this Investment Policy Statement, every quarter the Advisor shall review the portfolio and each asset class in which the Portfolio is invested. If the actual weighting differs from the target weighting by 5% or more from the recommended weighting (e.g., from a recommended 10% to less than 5% or more than 15% of total assets), the Advisor shall rebalance the portfolio back to the recommended weighting.

Adjustment in the Target Allocation

Should it become desirable for the endowment to become more or less aggressive with its investments, that would call for a change in the target allocation, as described above. When such a change needs to occur, it would only be made with the concurrence of the trustees, according to their bylaws.

Frequency of Review

The Investor recognizes that all investments go through cycles and, therefore, there will be periods of time in which the investment objectives are not met or when specific managers fail to meet their expected performance targets. Recognizing that no manager is perfect all the time and that good years help to make up for bad ones, the Investor acknowledges the principle that managers must be given an opportunity to make up for poor periods. Unless there are extenuating circumstances, patience will often prove appropriate when performance has been disappointing.

On an overall portfolio basis, the Investor establishes a goal of achieving the stated investment return objectives over a five-year period of time. A shorter time frame would contradict the principle that managers should generally be given the opportunity to overcome poor performance with subsequent excellent performance.

Liquidity

The Investor has determined that sufficient dependable income and liquidity are available from other sources such that the Investor does not need to maintain cash balances among these assets, except as may be dictated for investment or operational reasons.

Diversification

Investment of the Investor's funds shall be limited to individual marketable securities or packaged products (for example, mutual funds or unit investment trusts) in the following categories:

Permitted Asset Classes

1. Cash and cash equivalents
2. Fixed income–domestic bonds
3. Fixed income–non-U.S. bonds
4. Equities–U.S.
5. Equities–non-U.S.
6. Equities–emerging markets
7. Equities–REITs
8. Direct commercial real property ownership
9. Mortgages
10. Private equity opportunities

Permitted Security Types

1. Mutual funds–stocks, bonds, money market funds

2. Individual stocks, as long as they are traded on the New York, American or Nasdaq stock exchanges

3. Individual bonds, as long as they are rated A or better and traded on a major U.S. exchange (in other words, investment in high yield bonds and certain convertible bonds will be limited to the use of mutual funds)

4. Closed-end funds

5. Unit investment trusts

6. WEBS and other exchange traded funds

7. Covered call options

8. Venture capital

9. Bank certificates of deposit

Categories Excluded from Investment

The trustees specifically have directed that no investment shall be made by the Endowment in any limited partnership, unless the Endowment is also a general partner, or unless the vote of the trustees approves of the investment 100%.

Prohibited Asset Classes and/or Security Types

1. Precious metals

2. Short sales

3. Purchases of letter stock, private placements, or direct payments

4. Leveraged transactions

5. Commodities transactions

6. Puts, calls, straddles, or other option strategies, except as permitted above

Other Investment Considerations

No individual security, except diversified funds, shall make up more than 5% of the total Portfolio.

Selection/Retention Criteria for Investments

Investment Management Selection

Investment managers (including mutual funds, money managers and limited partnership sponsors) shall be chosen using the following criteria:

- Past performance, considered relative to other investments having the same investment objective. Consideration shall be given to both performance rankings over various time frames and consistency of performance.

- Costs relative to other funds with like objectives and investment styles.

- Size of the proposed mutual fund.

- Length of time the fund has been in existence and length of time it has been under the direction of the current manager(s) and whether or not there have been material changes in the manager's organization and personnel.

- The historical volatility and downside risk of each proposed investment.

- How well each proposed investment complements other assets in the Portfolio.

- The current economic environment.

- The likelihood of future investment success, relative to other opportunities.

Cash Equivalent Vehicles

All cash equivalent investments shall be pooled investment vehicles, such as money market funds, where the fund's share price is intended to remain constant and the fund's yield is comparable with the current risk-free rate of return. Also permitted in this category shall be United States agency-guaranteed bank certificates of deposit (purchased directly from banks or indirectly through brokerage accounts) or short-term U.S. government securities.

The following criteria for selecting and retaining any pooled investment vehicles serving as a cash-equivalent investment:

1. The fund will have an investment track record of no less than three years.

2. The fund's average annualized yield, net of fund level expenses, over a three-year period, will be no less than 0.5% below that of the average of all other funds sharing a similar investment objective for an equivalent period.

The Advisor, in conjunction with the Investor, will review the performance of each cash-equivalent vehicle on a quarterly basis. The investment vehicle's total returns will be compared with the average returns for all other cash-equivalent funds with a similar investment objective for the previous one-, three- and five-year periods.

In the event a selected fund underperforms the returns established by such averages by more than 0.5% for the prior three-year period, such fund(s) will be placed on probation for the subsequent twelve months. If over the subsequent one-year period the fund's average annual return remains 0.5% below that earned by the applicable average, the Advisor, in conjunction with the Investor, will make a determination as to whether the fund continues to be a prudent and appropriate investment.

Common Stocks

Any selected common stock funds shall be pooled investment vehicles, such as a publicly traded open or closed-end mutual fund, providing daily asset valuations. Such investments may include focus on any size domestic or non-U.S. stock.

The following criteria will be used for the selection and retention of any pooled common stock investment vehicles:

1. The fund will have an investment track record of no less than three years.

2. The fund's average annualized returns net of fund level expenses, over a three-year time period or more, will be no less than 20% below the average returns for equivalent pooled investment vehicles sharing the same investment objective.

3. The fund will incur investment risk no more than 20% above that incurred by publicly traded funds with the same investment objective, as measured by the fund's standard deviation.

The Advisor, in conjunction with the Investor, will review the performance of each common stock fund on a quarterly basis. Each fund's total returns will be compared against the average returns for equivalent pooled investment vehicles sharing the same investment objectives for the previous one-, three-, and five-year periods.

In the event any selection fund underperforms the applicable averages for a period of three years, the selection fund will be placed on probation for the subsequent twelve months. If over the subsequent year the fund's average return for the applicable three-year period remains below that earned by the average equivalent pooled investment vehicle sharing the same investment objective, the Advisor, in conjunction with the Investor, will make a determination as to whether the fund continues to be a prudent and appropriate investment.

The relative risk of the selected investment vehicle will also be reviewed on a quarterly basis, as measured by the fund's standard deviation, over the most recent one-, three-, and five-year periods. The fund's relative risk is to be calculated by independent fund evaluation services such as Lipper Analytical Services, Inc. or Morningstar, Inc.

In the event the level of risk assumed by the fund exceeds that incurred by the average for equivalent pooled investment vehicles sharing the same investment objectives by more than 20% over the previous three-year period, the Advisor, in conjunction with the Investor, will make a determination as to whether the fund continues to be a prudent and appropriate investment.

Bonds and Other Fixed Income Vehicles

Any selected diversified bond fund shall be pooled investment vehicles, such as a publicly traded mutual fund, providing net asset valuations published on a daily basis.

The following criteria will be used for the selection and retention of such diversified bond funds:

1. The fund will have an investment track record of no less than three years.

2. The fund's average annualized returns net of fund level expenses, over a three-year time period or more, will be no less than 20% below the average returns for equivalent pooled investment vehicles sharing the same investment objective.

3. The fund will incur investment risk no more than 20% above that incurred by publicly traded funds with the same investment objective, as measured by the fund's standard deviation.

4. The fund will invest in no fewer than twenty income-producing securities representing at least twenty corporate issuers or a comparable number of securities backed by the full faith and credit of the U.S. government or one of its agencies or a combination thereof.

The Advisor, in conjunction with the Investor, will review the performance of each fund on a quarterly basis. Each fund's total returns will be compared against the average returns for equivalent pooled investment vehicles sharing the same investment objectives for the previous one-, three-, and five-year periods.

In the event any selection fund underperforms the applicable averages for a period of three years, the selection fund will be placed on probation for the subsequent twelve months. If over the subsequent year the fund's average return for the applicable three-year period remains below that earned by the average equivalent pooled investment vehicle sharing the same investment objective, the Advisor, in conjunction with the Investor, will make a determination as to whether the fund continues to be a prudent and appropriate investment.

The relative risk of the selected investment vehicle will also be reviewed on a quarterly basis, as measured by the fund's standard deviation, over the most recent one-, three-, and five-year periods. The fund's relative risk is to be calculated by independent fund evaluation services such as Lipper Analytical Services, Inc. or Morningstar, Inc.

Investment Monitoring and Control Procedures

Reports

1. The investment custodian shall provide Investor with monthly statements for each account that list all assets held by Investor, values for each asset and all transactions affecting assets within the Portfolio, including additions and withdrawals.

2. Charitable Advisors, Inc. shall provide Investor no less frequently than on a quarterly basis and within 30 days within the end of each such quarter the following management reports:

   a) Portfolio performance results over the last quarter, year, 3 years and inception-to-date period

   b) Performance results of comparative benchmarks for the last quarter, year, 3 years and 5 years

   c) Performance results of each individual holding for the quarter

   d) Performance shall be reported on a basis that is in compliance with AIMR standards

e) End of quarter status regarding asset allocation—current versus policy

f) Any recommendations for changes of the above

Meetings and Communication

As a matter of course, Advisor shall keep Investor apprised of any material changes in Advisor's outlook, recommended investment policy, and tactics. In addition, Advisor shall meet with Investor approximately annually to review and explain the Portfolio's investment results and any related issues. Advisor shall also be available on a reasonable basis for telephone and e-mail communication as needed.

Any material event that affects the ownership of Advisor's firm or the management of the Portfolio must be reported immediately to Investor.

The Advisor

Advisor is expected to manage the Portfolio in a manner consistent with this Investment Policy Statement and in accordance with state and federal law and the Uniform Prudent Investor Act. Advisor is a registered investment adviser and shall act as the investment advisor and fiduciary to the Investor until the Investor decides otherwise.

Advisor shall be responsible for:

1. Designing, recommending and implementing an appropriate asset allocation plan consistent with the investment objectives, time horizon, risk profile, guidelines and constraints outlined in this statement

2. Recommending an appropriate custodian to safeguard Investor's assets

3. Advising the Investor about the selection of and the allocation of asset categories

4. Identifying specific assets and investment managers within each asset category

5. Ensuring that the custodian provides Investor with a current prospectus, where applicable, for each investment proposed for the portfolio

6. Monitoring the performance of all selected assets

7. Recommending changes to any of the above

8. Periodically reviewing the suitability of the investments for the Investor

9. Being available to meet with the Investor at least once each year, and being available at such other times within reason at the Investor's request

10. Preparing and presenting appropriate reports

Discretion and Title

● Advisor will not take title to any assets.

● Advisor shall be responsible only to make recommendations to the Investor and to implement investment decisions as directed by the Investor.

The Investor

Investor shall be responsible for:

1. The oversight of the Portfolio

2. Defining the investment objectives and policies of the Portfolio

3. Directing Advisor to make changes in investment policy and to oversee and to approve or disapprove Advisor's recommendations with regard to policy, guidelines, objectives and specific investments on a timely basis

4. Providing Advisor with all relevant information on Investor's financial conditions and risk tolerances and notifying Balanced Financial Advisors promptly of any changes to this information.

5. Reading and understanding the information contained in the prospectus and each investment in the Portfolio.

6. Exercising all rights, including voting rights, as are acquired through the purchase of securities.

Adoption

Adopted by the below signed:

Date:_____

Trustee(s):_____

_____

_____

Advisor:_____

Investment Policy Statement

Rock 'n' Roll Records Pension Plan

Dean L. Martin, Frank B. Sinatra and Sammy S. Davis, Jr.

September 1, 200X

Brash & Sassy Financial Advisors

Penthouse
Tallest Building in Town
New York, NY 10100

Table of Contents

Introduction

The purpose of this Investment Policy Statement (IPS) is to establish a clear understanding between Rock 'n' Roll Records Pension Plan ("Investor") and Brash & Sassy Financial Advisors ("Advisor") as to the investment goals and objectives and management policies applicable to the Investor's investment portfolio ("Portfolio"). This Investment Policy Statement will:

- Establish reasonable expectations, objectives and guidelines in the investment of the Portfolio's assets

- Create the framework for a well-diversified asset mix that can be expected to generate acceptable long-term returns at a level of risk suitable to the Investor, including:

  — describing an appropriate risk posture for the investment of the Investor's Portfolio

  — specifying the target asset allocation policy

  — establishing investment guidelines regarding the selection of investment managers, permissible securities and diversification of assets

  — specifying the criteria for evaluating the performance of the Portfolio's assets

- Define the responsibilities of the Investor and the Advisor

- Encourage effective communication between the investment manager(s) and the Investor

This IPS is not a contract. No legal counsel has reviewed this investment policy and the Advisor and Investor use it at their own discretion. This IPS is intended to be a summary of an investment philosophy and the procedures that provide guidance for the Investor and the Advisor. The investment policies described in this IPS should be dynamic. These policies should reflect the Investor's current status and philosophy regarding the investment of the Portfolio. These policies will be reviewed and revised periodically to ensure they adequately reflect any changes related to the Portfolio, to the Investor or the capital markets.

It is understood that there can be no guarantee about the attainment of the goals or investment objectives outlined herein.

Investment Policy Discussion

What Is an Investment Policy Statement?

An investment policy outlines and prescribes a prudent and acceptable investment philosophy and defines the investment management procedures and long-term goals for the Investor.

The Need for a Written Policy

The principal reason for developing a long-term investment policy and for putting it in writing is to enable you and us to protect your portfolio from ad hoc revisions of sound long-term policy. The written investment policy will help you maintain a long-term policy when short-term market movements may be distressing and the policy is in doubt.

The development of an investment policy follows the basic approach underlying financial planning: assessing your financial condition, setting goals, developing a strategy to meet the goals, implementing the strategy, regularly reviewing the results and adjusting the strategy or the implementation as circumstances dictate. Having and making use of an investment policy encourages you to become more disciplined and more systematic, thus improving the probability of satisfying your investment goals. The formal requirement for written investment policies originally arose out of regulations relating to company retirement plans (ERISA).

With the enactment of ERISA in 1974, trust fiduciaries became liable for breaches in prudence and diversification standards. ERISA 402(b)(1) states, "Every employee benefit trust shall provide a procedure for establishing and carrying out a funding policy and method consistent with the objectives of the trust and requirements of this title."

The Uniform Prudent Investor Act ("UPIA") was approved for use in all states at the 1994 annual Conference of Commissioners on Uniform State Law and by the American Bar Association in 1995. The act provides excellent guidance about the "prudent investment process."

Key provisions of the UPIA include:

- No investment is inherently prudent or imprudent, except in how its inclusion or exclusion impacts the portfolio as a whole.

- Trustees are expected to use all reasonably available strategies to improve the risk/reward relationship of the portfolio.

- Under most circumstances, the assets of the trust must be diversified.

- Trustees are obliged to spread portfolio investments across asset classes to enhance performance and reduce risk.

- The possible effect of inflation must be considered as part of the investment strategy. As a result, use of equities is encouraged to allow the possibility that the portfolio's growth will outpace inflation.

- Fiduciaries have a duty to either demonstrate investment skill in managing trust assets or to delegate investment management to another, more qualified party.

Steps to Take to Establish an Investment Policy

1. Assess your financial situation—identify your goals and your needs

2. Determine your tolerance for risk and your time horizon

3. Develop clear objectives for the trust

4. State how the investments are expected to help meet trust objectives

5. Identify any restrictions on the portfolio and its assets

6. Determine the asset classes and mix appropriate (the "Asset Allocation") to maximize the likelihood of achieving the investment objectives at the lowest level of risk

7. Determine the investment methodology to be used with regard to investment (manager) selection, rebalancing, buy-sell disciplines, portfolio reviews and reporting, etc.

8. Implement the decisions

9. Document all investment decisions

The net effort of the written policy is to increase the likelihood that the portfolio will be able to meet the financial needs of the Investor.

Overview Commentary

The Plan Sponsor

Rock 'n' Roll Records is now the third largest record company in the world. Created by big names from the past, it has signed more Top Ten artists in the last year than any other record company. Sales have been growing at 150% per year for the last five years and while much has been spent on infrastructure to support this and future growth, profits continue to be solid, even with the number of employees growing at 75% per year.

The pension plan was originally created for the three partners, but they have taken the position that as long as the company can afford it, they are happy to put aside similar contributions for current employees.

Plan Trustees

Dean L. Martin
Frank B. Sinatra
Sammy S. Davis, Jr.

Trust Data

Rock 'n' Roll Records created the pension plan on December 28, 1992. It was most recently amended on August 27, 2001. Plan year-end is 12/31 of each year. Its tax ID number is 87-6662222.

Employees Covered

Employees are eligible for contributions after one year of employment with Rock 'n' Roll Records. They must work at least 1000 hours in a plan (calendar year) for eligibility. No employee is currently excluded, except for the above two reasons, although there is a clause in the plan whereby unionized employees, who have their own retirement plans, would not also be eligible for this plan.

Vesting Schedule

Vesting is on a cliff basis. All contributions on an employee's behalf are fully vested after three years employment.

Distributions to Terminated Vested Participants

Vested amounts are to be distributed to former employees of Rock 'n' Roll Records within 45 days immediately following calendar year end. For example, if an employee were to leave in December, that employee should receive any distribution payments due or be eligible to roll distributions over by February 15 of the following year.

Actuarial Assumptions

These change from year to year and are provided by the plan administrator, Helga Goulag. Because of their changing nature, it was deemed inappropriate to make this part of the policy statement for investments.

Five-Year Cash-Flow Projections for the Plan

Projections are needed to help manage the cash-flow and to optimize the amounts invested. Cash that will be needed for distributions to employees who have left the firm should remain liquid, preferably in a money market account. Annual employer contributions to the plan are made in February of each year. It is anticipated that the contributions will generally be equal to or greater than the distributions in each plan. Therefore, there is minimal need to hold cash amounts aside to pay distributions. When, and if, the growth of the company levels off, it will be important to update these cash-flow projections at least annually.

	DISTRIBUTIONS	CONTRIBUTIONS	NET
Year 1	$50,000	$450,000	+$400,000
Year 2	$150,000	$1,200,000	+$1,050,000
Year 3	$300,000	$2,000,000	+$1,700,000
Year 4	$500,000	$3,000,000	+$2,500,000
Year 5	$750,000	$3,000,000	+$2,250,000

Key Contacts for Plan

Frank B. Sinatra, Chairman of the Board
Billy Joe Wilder, Chief Operating Officer

Jessica Parker, Director of Human Resources
Helga Goulag, President, Plans-R-Us
Ted Gotcha, CPA, Tax Preparation for the Trust

Fiduciary Bonding

The Rock Insurance Company 800-999-2222

Dollar Limit . . . . $5 million, or 15% of plan assets, whichever is greater

Bond Number A1B2C3D4

Economic Outlook

Rock 'n' Roll Records has been fortunate on a number of counts. Starting out with very recognizable names in the business helped establish them. Through their family contacts, they were able to sign a few of the newer stars early in their career and partly because of their own talent, and partly because of the support Rock 'n' Roll Records has been able to provide, they have become major talents. That, of course, brought more stars to the stable. The growth has allowed Rock 'n' Roll Records to develop a marketing and distribution system that is generally recognized as the best in the business.

The other favorable factor has been the growth in consumer willingness to pay higher prices for music, accompanied by video productions. National and world demographics support continued growth of the music business.

With the above in mind, Rock 'n' Roll Records forecasts continued growth, albeit probably not at the recent rates, for many years. That should allow continued contributions at increasing levels for quite a while.

Investment Philosophy

The basic tenets under which this portfolio will be managed include the following:

1. Modern portfolio theory, as recognized by the 1990 Nobel Prize, will be the primary influence driving the way the portfolio will be structured and how subsequent decisions will be made. The underlying concepts of modern portfolio theory include:

- Investors are risk averse. The only acceptable risk is that which is adequately compensated by potential portfolio returns.

- Markets are efficient. It is virtually impossible to know ahead of time the next direction of the market as a whole or of any individual security. It is, therefore, unlikely that any portfolio will succeed in consistently "beating the market."

- The portfolio as a whole is more important than an individual security. The appropriate allocation of capital among asset classes (stocks, bonds, cash, etc.) will have far more influence on long-term portfolio results than the selection of individual securities. Investing for the long term (preferably longer than ten years) becomes critical to investment success because it allows the long-term characteristics of the asset classes to surface.

- For every risk level, there exists an optimal combination of asset classes that will maximize returns. A diverse set of asset classes will be selected to help minimize risk. The proportionality of the mix of asset classes will determine the long-term risk and return characteristics of the portfolio as a whole.

- Portfolio risk can be decreased by increasing diversification of the portfolio and by lowering the correlation of market behavior among the asset classes selected. (Correlation is the statistical term for the extent to which two asset classes move in tandem or opposition to one another.)

2. Investing globally helps to minimize overall portfolio risk due to the imperfect correlation between economies of the world. Investing globally has also been shown historically to enhance portfolio returns, although there is no guarantee that it will do so in the future.

3. Equities offer the potential for higher long-term investment returns than cash or fixed income investments. Equities are also more volatile in their performance. Investors seeking higher rates of return must increase the proportion of equities in their portfolio, while at the same time accepting greater variation of results (including occasional declines in value).

4. Picking individual securities and timing the purchase or sale of investments in the attempt to "beat the market" are highly unlikely to increase long-term investment returns; they also can significantly increase portfolio operating costs. Such practices are, therefore, to be avoided.

5. The basic underlying approach to the management of this portfolio shall therefore be to optimize the risk/return relationship appropriate to Investor's needs and goals using a globally diverse portfolio of a variety of asset classes using mutual funds or managed portfolios, to "buy and hold" the selected securities and periodically re-optimize (rebalance).

Investment Objectives

The specific objectives for these assets shall be to achieve an average annual rate of return (over a period of five years) of the Consumer Price Index plus 4% for the aggregate investments under this Investment Policy Statement.

Time Horizon

Given that liquidity needs are minimal, as distributions are being easily offset by contributions, the time horizon for these investments is in excess of 10 years. Capital values do fluctuate over shorter periods and the Investor recognizes that the possibility of capital loss does exist. However, historical asset class return data suggest that the risk of principal loss over a holding period of at least three to five years can be minimized with the long-term investment mix employed under this Investment Policy Statement.

Tax Policy

This account is not subject to taxes, so all investment decisions are to be made without consideration of the tax impact.

Risk Tolerance

Investment theory and historical capital market return data suggest that, over long periods of time, there is a relationship between the level or risk assumed and the level of return that can be expected in an investment program. In general, higher risk (e.g., volatility of return) is associated with higher return.

The trustees are interested in seeing the value of assets grow over time, for the benefit of themselves and their employees. Being experienced investors, they understand that volatility comes with the desire for higher returns and are prepared to be patient through such periods.

At the same time, the trustees do not see any reason to take excessive risks. Taking these factors into account, the trustees have chosen to pursue a moderate risk investment policy. The trustees have indicated a willingness to tolerate declines in the value of this portfolio of between 0% and 10% in any given year. The Investor would accept losses as often as three out of ten times to achieve higher returns.

Asset Allocation

Academic research suggests that the decision to allocate total assets among various asset classes will far outweigh security selection and other decisions that affect portfolio performance. After reviewing the long-term performance and risk characteristics of various asset classes and balancing the risk and rewards of market behavior, the following asset classes were selected to achieve the objectives of the Investor's Portfolio.

ASSET ALLOCATION			
CATEGORY	HOLDINGS	PERCENT	TOTAL
Cash			2%
	Taxable Money Market Funds	2%	
Bonds			28%
	Intermediate-Term Gov't.	10%	
	High Grade Corporates	10%	
	High Yield Bonds	8%	
Stocks			54%
	Large Cap Stocks	25%	
	Small Cap Stocks	10%	
	International Stocks	15%	
	Emerging Market Stocks	4%	
Real Estate			16%
	Direct Real Estate Investments	12%	
	REITs	4%	
TOTAL		100%	100%

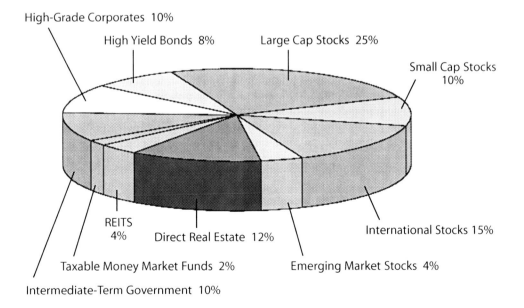

High-Grade Corporates 10%

High Yield Bonds 8%   Large Cap Stocks 25%

Small Cap Stocks 10%

REITS 4%   Direct Real Estate 12%

International Stocks 15%

Taxable Money Market Funds 2%   Emerging Market Stocks 4%

Intermediate-Term Government 10%

No guarantees can be given about future performance, and this Investment Policy Statement shall not be construed as offering such a guarantee.

It should be recognized that the Portfolio might invest in mutual funds. For such investments the actual weightings of these mutual funds and their holdings can and will vary. As a result, actual returns can be higher or lower than those presented below.

Solely for illustrative purposes, a portfolio of assets as described above, and combined in a manner consistent with the normalized weightings suggested above, and using standardized figures for each represented asset class based on historical norms and adjusted for today's environment, suggests that 95% of the time over the past thirty years, performance results have been within the following parameters:

Approximated Future Returns For Investor's Allocation Based on Asset Class Categories	ONE YEAR	TEN YEAR
Maximum for Period	36.5%	19.1%
Estimated Average	9.3%	9.3%
Minimum for Period	−8.5%	+2.3%
Worst-Case Conditions	−13.7%	−0.2%

All return calculations herein include price appreciation/depreciation, income distributions and capital gains distributions. Above figures based on 95% statistical likelihood, except for those of "Worst-Case Conditions," which returns are expected to exceed all but 0.5% of the time. Calculations do not include the impact of management fees or transaction costs.

On average, over long periods of time, this Portfolio design can be expected to experience losses one in five years, and in such cases should take an average of somewhat less than ten months to recover such losses. Over a five year period, such a portfolio's performance should exceed inflation 76% of the time.

Assumptions Used to Calculate Expected Returns

ASSET CLASS	EXPECTED RETURN	STANDARD DEVIATION
Money Market Funds	3.0%	2.0%
Intermediate-Term Gov't	5.6%	4.0%
High Grade Corporates	6.3%	4.9%
High Yield Bonds	8.9%	11.2%
Large Cap Stocks	11.1%	14.1%
Small Cap Stocks	12.4%	17.6%
International Stocks	10.9%	15.7%
Emerging Mkt Stocks	13.5%	23.4%
Direct Real Estate Invest.	10.2%	8.6%
REITs	10.6%	12.4%

Data used to develop assumptions have been provided by Ibbotson Associates and DFA Funds and have been based on the periods from 1972 to 200X, except emerging markets, which has available data from 1988.

Rebalancing Procedures

From time to time, market conditions may cause the Portfolio's investment in various asset classes to vary from the established allocation. To remain consistent with the asset allocation guidelines established by this Investment Policy Statement, every quarter the Advisor shall review the Portfolio and each asset class in which the Portfolio is invested. If the actual weighting differs from the target weighting by 5% or more from the recommended weighting (e.g., from a recommended 10% to less than 5% or more than 15% of total assets) the Advisor shall rebalance the Portfolio back to the recommended weighting.

Frequency of Review

The Investor recognizes that all investments go through cycles and, therefore, there will be periods of time in which the investment objectives are not met or when specific managers fail to meet their expected performance targets. Recognizing that no manager is perfect all the time and that good years help to make up for bad ones, the Investor acknowledges the principle that managers must be given an opportunity to make up for poor periods. Unless there are extenuating circumstances, patience will often prove appropriate when performance has been disappointing.

On an overall portfolio basis, the Investor establishes a goal of achieving the stated investment return objectives over a five-year period of time. A shorter time frame would contradict the principle that managers should generally be given the opportunity to overcome poor performance with subsequent excellent performance.

Liquidity

As indicated above, contributions have been and are expected to continue to exceed distributions substantially. Given that their timing is approximately the same, there is little need for liquidity, except for investment operational reasons.

Diversification

Investment of the Investor's funds shall be limited to individual marketable securities or packaged products (for example, mutual funds or unit investment trusts) in the following categories:

Permitted Asset Classes

1. Cash and cash equivalents

2. Fixed income–domestic bonds

3. Fixed income–non-U.S. bonds

4. Equities–U.S.

5. Equities–non-U.S.

6. Equities–emerging markets

7. Equities–REITs

8. Direct ownership of real estate

9. Mortgages

Permitted Security Types

1. Mutual funds–stocks, bonds, money market funds

2. Individual stocks, as long as they are traded on the New York, American or Nasdaq stock exchanges

3. Individual bonds, as long as they are rated A or better and traded on a major U.S. exchange

4. Closed-end funds

5. Unit investment trusts

6. WEBS and exchange traded funds

7. Investments in Limited Partnerships where the general partners have been known personally by the trustees for at least five years and whose primary business is the ownership of real estate.

8. Bank certificates of deposit

Categories Excluded from Investment

The trustees will not consider investing in any investment with which Arnie Schwartzenbaum is affiliated.

Prohibited Asset Classes and/or Security Types

1. Precious metals

2. Venture capital

3. Short sales

4. Purchases of letter stock, private placements, or direct payments

5. Leveraged transactions

6. Commodities transactions

7. Puts, calls, straddles, or other option strategies, except as permitted above

8. Purchases of real estate, with the exception of REITs

Other Investment Considerations

Other than index-based mutual funds, no investment shall exceed in value 5% of the total portfolio value.

Selection/Retention Criteria for Investments

Investment Management Selection

Investment managers (including mutual funds, money managers and limited partnership sponsors) shall be chosen using the following criteria:

- Past performance, considered relative to other investments having the same investment objective. Consideration shall be given to both performance rankings over various time frames and consistency of performance.

- Costs relative to other funds with like objectives and investment styles.

- Size of the proposed mutual fund.

- Length of time the fund has been in existence and length of time it has been under the direction of the current manager(s) and whether or not there have been material changes in the manager's organization and personnel.

- The historical volatility and downside risk of each proposed investment.

- How well each proposed investment complements other assets in the portfolio.

- The current economic environment.

- The likelihood of future investment success, relative to other opportunities.

Investment Monitoring and Control Procedures

Reports

1. Advisor shall provide Investor with a report each month that lists all assets held by Investor, values for each asset and all transactions affecting assets within the portfolio, including additions and withdrawals.

2. Investor shall receive no less frequently than on a quarterly basis, and within 30 days within the end of each such quarter, the following management reports:

   a) Portfolio performance results over the last quarter, year, 3 years and 5 years

   b) Performance results of each individual manager for the same periods

   c) Performance results of comparative benchmarks for the same periods

   d) Performance shall be reported on a basis that is in compliance with AIMR standards

e) End-of-quarter status regarding asset allocation—current versus policy

f) Any recommendations for changes of the above

Meetings and Communication Between Investor and Advisor

As a matter of course, Advisor shall keep Investor apprised of any material changes in the Advisor's outlook, recommended investment policy, and tactics. In addition, Advisor shall meet with Investor no less than annually (preferably semi-annually) to review and explain the Portfolio's investment results and any related issues. Advisor shall also be available on a reasonable basis for telephone communication when needed.

Any material event that affects the ownership of Advisor's firm or the management of the Portfolio must be reported immediately to Investor.

Duties and Responsibilities

The Advisor

Brash & Sassy Financial Advisors is expected to manage the Portfolio in a manner consistent with this Investment Policy Statement and in accordance with the Rock 'n' Roll Records Retirement Plan document, state and federal law and the Uniform Prudent Investor Act. Advisor is a Registered Investment Advisor and shall act as the investment advisor and fiduciary to the Investor until the Investor decides otherwise.

Advisor shall be responsible for:

1. Designing, recommending and implementing an appropriate asset allocation plan consistent with the investment objectives, time horizon, risk profile, guidelines and constraints outlined in this statement.

2. Recommending an appropriate custodian to safeguard Investor's assets.

3. Advising the Investor about the selection of and the allocation of asset categories.

4. Identifying specific assets and investment managers within each asset category.

5. Ensuring that the custodian provides Investor with a current prospectus, where applicable, for each investment proposed for the Portfolio.

6. Monitoring the performance of all selected assets.

7. Recommending changes to any of the above.

8. Advisor is responsible for and empowered to exercise all rights, including voting rights, as are acquired through the purchase of securities, where practical. Advisor shall vote proxies accordingly to the guidelines and restrictions outlined herein where applicable and otherwise according to Advisor's best judgment.

9. Periodically reviewing the suitability of the investments for the Investor being available to meet with the Investor at least twice each year, and being available at such other times within reason at the Investor's request.

10. Preparing and presenting appropriate reports.

Advisor will not take title to any assets nor shall Advisor exercise discretionary control over any of the Investor's assets. Advisor shall be responsible only to make recommendations to the Investor and to implement investment decisions as directed by the Investor.

The Investor

Investor shall be responsible for:

1. The oversight of the Portfolio.

2. Defining the investment objectives and policies of the Portfolio.

3. Directing Advisor to make changes in investment policy and to oversee and to approve or disapprove Advisor's recommendations

with regards to policy, guidelines, objectives and specific investments on a timely basis.

4. Providing Advisor with all relevant information on Investor's financial conditions and risk tolerances and notifying Advisor promptly
   of any changes to this information.

5. Reading and understanding the information contained in the
   prospectus and each investment in the Portfolio.

Adoption

Adopted by the below signed:

Date:_____

Trustee(s):_____

_____

_____

Advisor:_____

IPS Statement for a Profit Sharing Plan

Investment Policy Statement

Law Offices of Dooey, Howe & Cheetum Profit Sharing Plan

January 31, 200X

Williamson & Associates

515 Reno Street
New York, NY 11012

Table of Contents

Investment Policy Discussion

What Is an Investment Policy Statement?

An investment policy outlines and prescribes a prudent and acceptable investment philosophy and defines the investment management procedures and long-term goals for the Investor.

The Need for a Written Policy

The principal reason for developing a long-term investment policy and for putting it in writing is to enable you and us to protect your portfolio from ad hoc revisions of sound long-term policy. The written investment policy will help you maintain a long-term policy when short-term market movements may be distressing and the policy is in doubt.

The development of an investment policy follows the basic approach underlying financial planning: assessing your financial condition, setting goals, developing a strategy to meet the goals, implementing the strategy, regularly reviewing the results and adjusting the strategy or the implementation as circumstances dictate. Having and making use of an investment policy encourages you to become more disciplined and more systematic, thus improving the probability of satisfying your investment goals. The formal requirement for written investment policies originally arose out of regulations relating to company retirement plans (ERISA).

The Uniform Prudent Investor Act ("UPIA") was approved for use in all states at the 1994 annual Conference of Commissioners on Uniform State Law and by the American Bar Association in 1995. The act is applicable to all irrevocable trusts, bypass trusts, QTIPs, ILITs, CRTs, QPRTs, QDTs, and GRTs. Noncompliance with these rules can expose a trustee to significant personal liability. Being clear about the intents, purposes and processes of the trust goes a long way toward protecting the trustee and helping the beneficiaries have clear and appropriate expectations.

Key provisions of the UPIA include:

- No investment is inherently prudent or imprudent, except in how its inclusion or exclusion impacts the portfolio as a whole.

- Trustees are expected to use all reasonably available strategies to improve the risk/reward relationship of the portfolio.

- Under most circumstances, the assets of the trust must be diversified.

- Trustees are obliged to spread portfolio investments across asset classes to enhance performance and reduce risk.

- The possible effect of inflation must be considered as part of the investment strategy. As a result, use of equities is encouraged to allow the possibility that the portfolio's growth will outpace inflation.

- Fiduciaries have a duty to either demonstrate investment skill in managing trust assets or to delegate investment management to another, more qualified party.

Steps to Take to Establish an Investment Policy

1. Assess your financial situation—identify your goals and your needs

2. Determine your tolerance for risk and your time horizon

3. Develop clear objectives for the trust

4. State how the investments are expected to help meet trust objectives

5. Identify any restrictions on the portfolio and its assets

6. Determine the asset classes and mix appropriate (the "Asset Allocation") to maximize the likelihood of achieving the investment objectives at the lowest level of risk

7. Determine the investment methodology to be used with regards to investment (manager) selection, rebalancing, buy-sell disciplines, portfolio reviews and reporting, etc.

8. Implement the decisions

9. Document all investment decisions

The net effort of the written policy is to increase the likelihood that the portfolio will be able to meet the financial needs of the Investor.

Introduction

The purpose of this Investment Policy Statement (IPS) is to establish a clear understanding between the trustees of the Law Offices of Dooey, Howe & Cheetum Profit Sharing Plan ("Investor") and Williamson & Associates ("Advisor") as to the investment goals and objectives and management policies applicable to the Investor's investment portfolio ("Portfolio"). This Investment Policy Statement will:

- Establish reasonable expectations, objectives and guidelines in the investment of the Portfolio's assets

- Create the framework for a well-diversified asset mix that can be expected to generate acceptable long-term returns at a level of risk suitable to the Investor, including:

  — describing an appropriate risk posture for the investment of the Investor's Portfolio

  — specifying the target asset allocation policy

  — establishing investment guidelines regarding the selection of investment managers, permissible securities and diversification of assets

  — specifying the criteria for evaluating the performance of the Portfolio's assets

- Define the responsibilities of the Investor and the Advisor

- Encourage effective communication between the investment manager(s) and the Investor

This IPS is not a contract. This investment policy has not been reviewed by any legal counsel and the Advisor and Investor use it at their own discretion. This IPS is intended to be a summary of an investment philosophy and the procedures that provide guidance for the Investor and the Advisor. The investment policies described in this IPS should be dynamic. These policies should reflect the Investor's current status and philosophy regarding the investment of the Portfolio. These policies will be reviewed and revised periodically to ensure they adequately reflect any changes related to the Portfolio, to the Investor or the capital markets.

It is understood that there can be no guarantee about the attainment of the goals or investment objectives outlined herein.

The Plan Sponsor . . . . Law Offices of Dooey, Howe & Cheetum

Plan Trustees . . . . Louie Dooey and Summer Some Howe

Trust Federal Tax Identification Numbers 77-6166888

Plan Year End . . . . December 31

Key Contacts for Plan . . . . Plan Administrator
Teri Mortensen
Mortensen & Associates
(212) 529-0000

Overview Commentary

The plan sponsor (Law Offices of Dooey, Howe & Cheetum) is the successor firm to the Law Offices of Phillum, Dooey, Howe & Cheetum. The prior firm had built up assets in excess of $1.5 million. At the split-up of the firm into two parts in mid-1998, the funds were disbursed based on where the former participants were subsequently employed: with Dooey, Howe & Cheetum, with Phillum or elsewhere. This plan represents those assets now associated with Mr. Dooey, Ms. Howe, Mr. Cheetum, and the other plan participants of their firm, plus any additional contributions made to the current plan.

Client Information

Trustees: . . . . .Louie Dooey and Summer Some Howe

Client . . . .Law Offices of Dooey, Howe & Cheetum Profit Sharing Plan
1651 I Street, Suite 150
New York, NY 10011
(212) 521-2500

Account Information

Investment Account . . . . .Law Offices of Dooey, Howe & Cheetum
Profit Sharing Plan

Custodian . . . . Charles Schwab & Co.

Account Number 5555-6789

Tax ID Number 77-6166888

Authorized Decision Makers . . . Louie Dooey and Summer Some Howe

Account Value $1,150,000

Investment Advisor . . . . Williamson & Associates
515 Reno Street
New York, NY 11012

Investment Philosophy

The basic tenets under which this portfolio will be managed include the following:

1. Modern portfolio theory, as recognized by the 1990 Nobel Prize, will be the primary influence driving the way the portfolio will be structured and how subsequent decisions will be made. The underlying concepts of modern portfolio theory include:

    - Investors are risk averse. The only acceptable risk is that which is adequately compensated by potential portfolio returns.

    - Markets are efficient. It is virtually impossible to know ahead of time the next direction of the market as a whole or of any individual security. It is, therefore, unlikely that any portfolio will succeed in consistently "beating the market."

- The portfolio as a whole is more important than an individual security. The appropriate allocation of capital among asset classes (stocks, bonds, cash, etc.) will have far more influence on long-term portfolio results than the selection of individual securities. Investing for the long term (preferably longer than ten years) becomes critical to investment success because it allows the long-term characteristics of the asset classes to surface.

- For every risk level, there exists an optimal combination of asset classes that will maximize returns. A diverse set of asset classes will be selected to help minimize risk. The proportionality of the mix of asset classes will determine the long-term risk and return characteristics of the portfolio as a whole.

- Portfolio risk can be decreased by increasing diversification of the portfolio and by lowering the correlation of market behavior among the asset classes selected. (Correlation is the statistical term for the extent to which two asset classes move in tandem or opposition to one another.)

2. Investing globally helps to minimize overall portfolio risk due to the imperfect correlation between economies of the world. Investing globally has also been shown historically to enhance portfolio returns, although there is no guarantee that it will do so in the future.

3. Equities offer the potential for higher long-term investment returns than cash or fixed income investments. Equities are also more volatile in their performance. Investors seeking higher rates of return must increase the proportion of equities in their portfolio, while at the same time accepting greater variation of results (including occasional declines in value).

4. Picking individual securities and timing the purchase or sale of investments in the attempt to "beat the market" are highly unlikely to increase long-term investment returns; they also can significantly

increase portfolio operating costs. Such practices are, therefore, to be avoided.

5. The basic underlying approach to the management of this portfolio shall therefore be to optimize the risk/return relationship appropriate to Investor's needs and goals using a globally diverse portfolio of a variety of asset classes using mutual funds or managed portfolios, to "buy and hold" the selected securities and periodically re-optimize (rebalance).

Investment Objectives

The specific objectives for these assets shall be to achieve an average annual rate of return (over a period of ten years) of the Consumer Price Index plus 5% for the aggregate investments under this Investment Policy Statement.

Time Horizon

For the purposes of planning, the time horizon for these investments is to be in excess of ten years. Capital values do fluctuate over shorter periods and the Investor should recognize that the possibility of capital loss does exist. However, historical asset-class-return data suggest that the risk of principal loss over a holding period of at least three to five years can be minimized with the long-term investment mix employed under this Investment Policy Statement.

Risk Tolerance

Investment theory and historical capital market return data suggest that, over long periods of time, there is a relationship between the level or risk assumed and the level of return that can be expected in an investment program. In general, higher risk (e.g., volatility of return) is associated with higher return.

277

Given this relationship between risk and return, a fundamental step in determining the investment policy for the Portfolio is the determination of an appropriate risk tolerance. There are two primary factors that affect the Investor's risk tolerance:

- Financial ability to accept risk within the investment program
- Willingness to accept return volatility

Taking these two factors into account, the Investor rates his or her own risk tolerance as moderate. The Investor recognizes that higher returns involve some volatility and has indicated a willingness to tolerate declines in the value of this portfolio of between 0% and 10% in a given year. The Investor would accept losses as often as two out of ten times to achieve higher returns.

Asset Allocation

Academic research suggests that the decision to allocate total assets among various asset classes will far outweigh security selection and other decisions that affect portfolio performance. After reviewing the long-term performance and risk characteristics of various asset classes and balancing the risk and rewards of market behavior, the following asset classes were selected to achieve the objectives of the Investor's Portfolio.

ASSET ALLOCATION			
CATEGORY	HOLDINGS	PERCENT	TOTAL
Cash			**4%**
	Taxable Money Market Funds	4%	
Bonds			**26%**
	High Grade Corporates	6%	
	High Yield Bonds	5%	
	International Bonds	5%	
	Mortgage Loan	10%	
Stocks			**65%**
	Large Cap Stocks	20%	
	Small Cap Stocks	10%	
	International Stocks	16%	
	Emerging Market Stocks	5%	
	Balanced	14%	
Real Estate			**5%**
	REITs	5%	
TOTAL		**100%**	**100%**

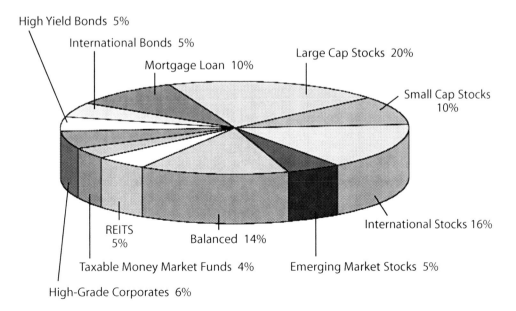

High Yield Bonds 5%

International Bonds 5%

Mortgage Loan 10%

Large Cap Stocks 20%

Small Cap Stocks 10%

International Stocks 16%

REITS 5%

Balanced 14%

Emerging Market Stocks 5%

Taxable Money Market Funds 4%

High-Grade Corporates 6%

No guarantees can be given about future performance, and this Investment Policy Statement shall not be construed as offering such a guarantee.

It should be recognized that the Portfolio will invest in mutual funds; that the actual weightings of these mutual funds can and will vary. As a result, actual returns can be higher or lower than those presented below.

Solely for illustrative purposes, a portfolio of assets (exclusive of any funds which may be managed elsewhere) combined in a manner consistent with the normalized weightings suggested above and using standardized figures for each represented asset class based on historical norms and adjusted for today's environment suggests that 95% of the time, performance results can be reasonably projected as follows:

Approximated Future Returns	
For Investor's Allocation Based on Asset Class Categories	
	ONE YEAR
Maximum for Period	31.56%
Estimated Average	9.14%
Minimum for Period	−14.78%
Worst-Case Conditions	−25.99%

All return calculations herein include price appreciation/depreciation, income distributions and capital gains distributions. Above figures based on 95% statistical likelihood, except for those of "Worst-Case Conditions," which returns are expected to exceed all but 5% of the time. Calculations do not include the impact of management fees, transaction costs or taxes.

Updated Allocations

From time to time, it may be desirable to amend the basic allocation policy or calculations. When such changes are made, updates will be attached to this Investment Policy Statement as an Appendix and will be considered part of this Investment Policy Statement.

Rebalancing Procedures

From time to time, market conditions may cause the Portfolio's investment in various asset classes to vary from the established allocation. To remain consistent with the asset allocation guidelines established by this Investment Policy Statement, every quarter the Advisor shall review the portfolio and each asset class in which the Portfolio is invested. If the actual weighting differs from the target weighting by 5% or more from the recommended weighting (e.g., from a recommended 10% to less than 5% or more than 15% of total assets), the Advisor shall rebalance the portfolio back to the recommended weighting.

Frequency of Review

The investor recognizes that all investments go through cycles and, therefore, there will be periods of time in which the investment objectives are not met or when specific managers fail to meet their expected performance targets. Recognizing that no manager is perfect all the time and that good years help to make up for bad ones, the Investor acknowledges the principle that managers must be given an opportunity to make up for poor periods. Unless there are extenuating circumstances, patience will often prove appropriate when performance has been disappointing.

On an overall portfolio basis, the Investor establishes a goal of achieving the stated investment return objectives over a five-year period of time. A shorter time frame would contradict the principle that managers should generally be given the opportunity to overcome poor performance with subsequent excellent performance.

Liquidity

The Investor has determined that sufficient dependable income and liquidity are available from other sources such that the Investor does not need to maintain cash balances among these assets, except as may be dictated for investment or operational reasons.

Marketability of Assets

Due to the Investor's relatively long-term investment horizon, the Investor has determined that up to 15% of the assets under this Investment Policy Statement can be invested in illiquid, long-term investments. Such investments may include, but shall not be limited to, deferred annuities, private real estate investment trusts, limited partnerships and bank certificates of deposit with extended maturities.

Diversification

Investment of the Investor's funds shall be limited to individual marketable securities or packaged products (for example, mutual funds or unit investment trusts) in the following categories:

Permitted Asset Classes

1. Cash and cash equivalents
2. Fixed income–domestic bonds
3. Fixed income–non-U.S. bonds
4. Equities–U.S.
5. Equities–non-U.S.
6. Equities–emerging markets
7. Equities–REITs
8. Mortgages

Permitted Security Types

1. Mutual funds–stocks, bonds, money market funds
2. Individual stocks, as long as they are traded on the New York, American or Nasdaq stock exchanges
3. Individual bonds, as long as they are rated A or better and traded on a major U.S. exchange

4. Closed-end funds

5. Unit investment trusts

6. Investments in limited partnerships

7. Bank certificates of deposit

Prohibited Asset Classes and/or Security Types

1. Covered call options

2. Deferred annuities issued by an insurance company

3. Equipment leasing

4. Precious metals

5. Venture capital

6. Short sales

7. Purchases of letter stock, private placements, or direct payments

8. Leveraged Transactions

9. Commodities Transactions

10. Puts, calls, straddles, or other option strategies, except as permitted above

11. Purchases of real estate, with the exception of REITs

Selection/Retention Criteria for Investments

Investment Management Selection

Investment managers (including mutual funds, money managers and limited partnership sponsors) shall be chosen using the following criteria:

- Past performance, considered relative to other investments having the same investment objective. Consideration shall be given to both performance rankings over various time frames and consistency of performance.

- Costs relative to other funds with like objectives and investment styles.

- Size of the proposed mutual fund.

- Length of time the fund has been in existence and length of time it has been under the direction of the current manager(s) and whether or not there have been material changes in the manager's organization and personnel.

- The historical volatility and downside risk of each proposed investment.

- How well each proposed investment complements other assets in the Portfolio.

- The current economic environment.

- The likelihood of future investment success, relative to other opportunities.

Investment Monitoring and Control Procedures

Reports

1. Advisor shall provide Investor with a report each month that lists all assets held by Investor, values for each asset and all transactions affecting assets within the Portfolio, including additions and withdrawals.

2. Investor shall receive no less frequently than on a quarterly basis, and within 30 days within the end of each such quarter, the following management reports:

   a) Portfolio performance results over the last quarter, year, 3 years and 5 years

   b) Performance results of each individual manager for the same periods

   c) Performance results of comparative benchmarks for the same periods

d) Performance shall be reported on a basis that is in compliance with AIMR standards

e) End-of-quarter status regarding asset allocation—current versus policy

f) Any recommendations for changes of the above

Meetings and Communication Between Investor and Advisor

As a matter of course, Advisor shall keep Investor apprised of any material changes in the Advisor's outlook, recommended investment policy, and tactics. In addition, Advisor shall meet with Investor no less than annually (preferably semi-annually) to review and explain the Portfolio's investment results and any related issues. Advisor shall also be available on a reasonable basis for telephone communication when needed.

Any material event that affects the ownership of Advisor's firm or the management of the Portfolio must be reported immediately to Investor.

Duties and Responsibilities

The Advisor

Advisor is expected to manage the Portfolio in a manner consistent with this Investment Policy Statement and in accordance with State and Federal law and the Uniform Prudent Investor Act. Advisor is a Registered Investment Advisor and shall act as the investment advisor and fiduciary to the Investor until the Investor decides otherwise.

Williamson & Associates shall be responsible for:

1. Designing, recommending and implementing an appropriate asset allocation plan consistent with the investment objectives, time horizon, risk profile, guidelines and constraints outlined in this statement.

2. Recommending an appropriate custodian to safeguard Investor's assets.

3. Advising the Investor about the selection of and the allocation of asset categories.

4. Identifying specific assets and investment managers within each asset category.

5. Ensuring that the custodian provides Investor with a current prospectus, where applicable, for each investment proposed for the Portfolio.

6. Monitoring the performance of all selected assets.

7. Recommending changes to any of the above.

8. Advisor is responsible for and empowered to exercise all rights, including voting rights, as are acquired through the purchase of securities, where practical. Advisor shall vote proxies accordingly to the guidelines and restrictions outlined herein where applicable and otherwise according to Advisor's best judgment.

9. Periodically reviewing the suitability of the investments for the Investor

10. Being available to meet with the Investor at least twice each year, and being available at such other times within reason at the Investor's request.

11. Preparing and presenting appropriate reports.

Advisor will not take title to any assets nor shall Advisor exercise discretionary control over any of the Investor's assets. Advisor shall be responsible only to make recommendations to the Investor and to implement investment decisions as directed by the Investor.

The Investor

Law Offices of Dooey, Howe & Cheetum Profit Sharing Plan
shall be responsible for:

1. The oversight of the Portfolio.

2. Defining the investment objectives and policies of the Portfolio.

3. Directing Advisor to make changes in investment policy and to oversee and to approve or disapprove Advisor's recommendations with regards to policy, guidelines, objectives and specific investments on a timely basis.

4. Providing Advisor with all relevant information on Investor's financial conditions and risk tolerances and notifying Advisor promptly of any changes to this information.

5. Reading and understanding the information contained in the prospectus and each investment in the Portfolio.

Adoption

Adopted by the below signed:

Date:_____

Trustee(s):_____

_____

Advisor:_____

IPS Executive Summary for File

D,H&C P/S Plan

Original IPS Date: January 31, 2003

Amended on: _____

Investor . . . Law Offices of Dooey, Howe & Cheetum Profit Sharing Plan
Louie Dooey and Summer Some Howe, Trustees

Tax ID Number 77-6166888

Custodian: . . . . Charles Schwab & Co.
Account #5555-6789

Investment Objective: average annual rate of return of the Consumer Price Index plus 5%

Time Horizon: In excess of ten years

ASSET ALLOCATION	
Money Market Funds	4%
Corporate Bonds	6%
High Yield Bonds	5%
International Bonds	5%
Private First Morgage	10%
U.S. Large Stocks	20%
U.S. Small Stocks	10%
International Stocks	16%
Emerging Market Stocks	5%
REITs	5%
Balanced Funds	14%
TOTAL	100%

Risk Tolerance: Risk tolerance rated as moderate. The Investor has indicated a willingness to tolerate declines in the value of this portfolio of between 0% and 10% in a given year. The Investor would accept losses as often as two out of ten times to achieve higher returns.

Expected Range of Returns for Selected Asset Allocation	
	ONE YEAR
Maximum Expected Return for Period	31.56%
Estimated Average Expected Return	9.14%
Minimum Expected Return for Period	−14.78%
Worst-Case Expected Return for Period	−25.99%

Investment Policy Statement

Acme Company 401(k) Plan

Susan Thompson, Trustee
William Holden, Trustee
Richard L. Dreyfus, Trustee

September 1, 200X

Ace Checkwriter, Financial Advisors

6677 Temple Street
Philadelphia, PA 11001
(999) 444-1111

Table of Contents

Introduction

The purpose of this Investment Policy Statement (IPS) is to establish a clear understanding between Acme 401(k) plan trustees ("Investor") and Ace Checkwriter, Financial Advisors ("Advisor") as to the investment goals and objectives and management policies applicable to the Investor's investment portfolio ("Portfolio"). This Investment Policy Statement will:

- Establish reasonable expectations, objectives and guidelines in the investment of the Portfolio's assets

- Create the framework for a well-diversified asset mix that can be expected to generate acceptable long-term returns at a level of risk suitable to the Investor, including:

  — describing an appropriate risk posture for the investment of the Investor's Portfolio

  — specifying the target asset allocation policy

  — establishing investment guidelines regarding the selection of investment managers, permissible securities and diversification of assets

  — specifying the criteria for evaluating the performance of the Portfolio's assets

- Define the responsibilities of the Investor and the Advisor

- Encourage effective communication between the investment manager(s) and the Investor

This IPS is not a contract. This investment policy has not been reviewed by any legal counsel and the Advisor and Investor use it at their own discretion. This IPS is intended to be a summary of an investment philosophy and the procedures that provide guidance for the Investor and the Advisor. The investment policies described in this IPS should be dynamic. These policies should reflect the Investor's current status and philosophy regarding the investment of the Portfolio. These policies will be reviewed and revised periodically to ensure they adequately reflect any changes related to the Portfolio, to the Investor or the capital markets.

It is understood that there can be no guarantee about the attainment of the goals or investment objectives outlined herein.

Investment Policy Discussion

What Is an Investment Policy Statement?

An investment policy outlines and prescribes a prudent and acceptable investment philosophy and defines the investment management procedures and long-term goals for the Investor.

The Need for a Written Policy

The principal reason for developing a long-term investment policy and for putting it in writing is to enable you and us to protect your portfolio from ad hoc revisions of sound long-term policy. The written investment policy will help you maintain a long-term policy when short-term market movements may be distressing and the policy is in doubt.

With the enactment of ERISA (Employee Retirement Income Security Act) in 1974, trust fiduciaries became liable for breaches in prudence and diversification standards. ERISA 402(b)(1) states, "Every employee benefit trust shall provide a procedure for establishing and carrying out a funding policy and method consistent with the objectives of the trust and requirements of this title." Noncompliance with these rules can expose a trustee to significant personal liability. Being clear about the intents, purposes and processes of the trust goes a long way toward protecting the trustee and helping the beneficiaries have clear and appropriate expectations.

The purpose of an Investment Policy Statement for a self-directed 401(k) plan has to do more with the structure of the plan than the implementation of the policies in an investment portfolio. In a self-directed 401(k) plan, employees are free to choose how to invest their money and generally the employer's contributions, within the parameters set forth by the trustees. In some self-directed 401(k) plans, there are virtually no limits and employees can choose from the full universe of legally acceptable investments; in others the choices may be limited to three to five mutual funds. Regardless of the limits, this Investment Policy Statement is not intended to direct how the employees choose to invest, but rather to guide the decisions of the trustees with regards to the plan and its offerings.

Overview Commentary

404(c)

The Acme Company 401(k) plan is a self-directed 401(k) plan. It is the intent of Acme Company and its plan trustees to comply with the requirements of Section 404(c) of the Internal Revenue Code to obtain "safe harbor" from potential penalties to the employer related to self-directed investment accounts.

The Plan Sponsor

Acme Company
123 Main Street
Mizzoula, Montana 88080
(555) 777-9999

Plan Trustees

Susan Thompson, President
William Holden, Director of Human Resources
Richard L. Dreyfus, Legal Counsel

Trust Data

The Acme Company Retirement Plan was created on May 15, 1997, and most recently amended on December 12, 2001. The plan year corresponds with the calendar year, and ends on December 31 of each year.

Trust assets as of 12/31/200X were $3,500,023.

Employer match: 75% of the first 4% contributed. For example, 3% match for a 4% deferral.

Other items:

- Profits are not required in order for Acme Company to make contributions to the Acme Company Retirement Plan

- Normal retirement age for plan participants is 65

- Loans are available from both non-profit-sharing contributions and profit-sharing contributions

Employees Covered

All employees of Acme Company, except unionized employees, are covered under the Acme Company Retirement Plan. Employees are eligible to participate effective the start of any calendar quarter after they have been employed by Acme for at least three months. Only employees working half-time or more are eligible.

Vesting Schedule

All payroll deductions are 100% vested immediately, since it is the employee's money to begin with.

Employer contributions will be vested according to the following schedule:

> 20% after one year of service to Acme
> 40% after two years of service to Acme
> 60% after three years of service to Acme
> 80% after four years of service to Acme
> 100% after five years of service to Acme

Any forfeited amounts (unvested dollars left by terminating employees) shall be proportionally divided among the employee accounts remaining in the plan as of the date of termination and subject to the same vesting schedule as any other employer contribution.

Distributions to Terminated Vested Participants

Terminated plan participants shall receive their own contributions, any vested employer contributions and any growth related thereto no later than 120 days after the date of termination.

Key Contacts for Plan

Plan Administrator:
EZTrader 333-252-5692

Administrator shall be responsible for keeping trust documents in compliance with current laws, for providing quarterly reports to all participants, and for preparing appropriate tax returns and other compliance documents.

Accountant:
Tax Avoidance, Inc. . . . . 6400 Temple Street, #2050
Philadelphia, PA 11001
(999) 444-3333

Accountant shall review all tax returns prior to being filed by trustees and shall assist sponsor in taking full tax advantage of the plan.

Investment Advisor:
Deborah Manligirl, EZTrader 333-444-5555

Investment Advisor shall act as a co-trustee to the plan, providing on-going strategic investment advice, specific investment recommendations, and quarterly performance reports showing absolute and comparative performance figures. Investment Advisor shall be considered a fiduciary to this plan.

Fiduciary Bonding:
Travelers ($500,000 Limit)
Policy # 077BZ10780573xaBCM

Other Information

Custodian . . . . Bank of America Securities

Account Number 34567-23

Tax ID Number 55-9876543

Authorized Decision Maker . . . . Plan Trustees

Investment Advisor . . . . Ace Checkwriter, Financial Advisors
6677 Temple Street
Philadelphia, PA 11001
(999) 444-1111

Fiduciary Responsibility

Plan trustees and other fiduciaries have a number of responsibilities when overseeing a self-directed 401(k)/profit sharing retirement plan.

One of the first decisions needs to be whether or not the plan will be safe-harbored under 404(c) regulations. Under 404(c) regulations, 401(k) plan participants must be given reasonable investment choices and provided with the tools to help them make appropriate investment decisions. Only when such is the case can fiduciaries avoid responsibility for investment results brought about by the decisions made by plan participants. For the fiduciaries to be so protected, they must clearly state they wish to abide by this regulation and then must meet the following standards:

1. Investment choices must be prudently selected and represent a broad range of options. This is interpreted to mean there must be no less than three distinctly different choices, in terms of risk and reward—usually at minimum, cash or fixed income, stocks and bonds.

2. Participants must have available, on an ongoing basis, information on the suitability and performance of each choice. At minimum this should be available quarterly and should include comparative numbers or benchmarks to assist in investment evaluation.

3. Full and adequate disclosure about possible investment costs, volatility, losses and market fluctuations must be available to participants to help them make educated investment choices.

4. The investment choices must be well diversified themselves. This will typically require that mutual funds or other pooled investment vehicles be used.

5. Participants must have the right to change their investment selections and transfer funds between investment choices at least quarterly to allow them to address current market conditions.

While these are good guidelines in any case, trustees must also address other issues. On the investment side, the development of an Investment Policy Statement will help the trustees determine what investment options to offer and how to make those decisions. They should also decide how they will make decisions about replacing an investment choice. They will need to decide about reporting and education procedures. They also need to oversee the party doing the record-keeping (usually contracted to a specialist).

The Acme Company Retirement Plan has been created for the dual purposes of (1) helping employees save and prepare for retirement in a tax-favored way and (2) sharing the wealth or profits generated by the efforts of each of our employees.

It is the intent of Acme Company that each employee should have the right to decide how much to contribute to the plan on their own behalf and how to invest not only those amounts but also any amounts contributed by Acme for the benefit of that employee. To assist participants as they make investment decisions, Acme intends to provide regular information and training to plan participants.

Investment choices allowed to plan participants will be varied enough and selected with enough care that it will be readily possible for any plan participant to choose to create a prudent, diversified portfolio.

Each Plan participant must be permitted to exercise control over assets in his or her account. The plan participants are responsible for making their own investment decisions and bear the risk of the investments that they have selected. Participants are also responsible for re-allocating assets according to their personal circumstances and risk tolerance. These requirements must be met for the participant to exercise control.

Participants:

- Must have the opportunity to choose from a wide range of investment options, consisting of at least three categories with varying risk and return characteristics

- Must have the ability to diversify investments generally and within investment categories

- Must be able to develop an investment portfolio with risk and return characteristics appropriate to their own financial and personal circumstances

- Must have the opportunity to materially affect the risk and return of their own accounts and to diversify investments so as to minimize the risk of large losses

- Must be able to transfer assets from one investment to another at intervals reasonably commensurate with the volatility of the underlying investments

- Absent any definition of "reasonably commensurate," must be able to switch at least once in any three-month period

Participants must be able to give instructions to, and receive written confirmation from, an identified fiduciary who is obligated to carry out the instructions. Participants must be provided with, or have the opportunity to obtain, sufficient information to make an informed investment decision.

Disclosure Requirements

The trustees have a duty to disclose to participants the following on a periodic basis:

- An explanation that the plan is intended to meet the requirements of Section 404(c) and that the plan fiduciaries will be relieved of liability for investment loss resulting from the participant's investments

- A description of the available investment alternatives, including investment objectives, risk and return characteristics, type of assets, and diversification of the Portfolios

- Identification of any designated investment managers

- Procedures on how to give investment instructions, including a description of any limitations on investment changes and any restrictions on voting and tender rights

- A description of any fees, expenses, or charges to participants' accounts in connection with any transaction, including sales load, commissions, redemption fees, etc.

- The name, address, and telephone number of the plan fiduciary, or the designated agent for the purpose of providing information on demand

- If an investment alternative includes employer securities, the plan procedures designated to ensure confidentiality, and the name, address, and telephone number of the plan fiduciary responsible for monitoring compliance with the confidentiality procedures

- A copy of the most recent prospectus for investment alternatives subject to the Securities Act of 1933

- Any material received by the plan, regarding voting, tender and similar rights to the extent those rights are passed through to participants

The plan trustees must provide the following information to plan participants upon demand:

- A description of the annual expenses of the investment alternatives

- Copies of any prospectuses, financial statements or reports, or other materials relating to the investment alternatives supplied to the plan

- Copies of the portfolios or lists of assets of the investment alternatives, including the value of each asset or the name and address of the issuer of any fixed rate contract

- Information relating to the value of the shares or units of the investment alternatives and past and current investment performance net of expenses

- Information on the value of the share or units in the participant's individual account

Each plan participant will be provided the following:

- Web access on a daily basis, providing up to date information about the choices they've made and the value of their investments

- Quarterly summary statements of their accounts

- Quarterly economic and market reviews

- Annual updates on the investment choices
- Annual copies of the Summary Plan Description

Investment Choices

Academic research suggests that the decision to allocate total assets among various asset classes will far outweigh security selection and other decisions that affect portfolio performance. The plan trustees therefore believe it is necessary and desirable that each employee have a range of choices, allowing them to construct or choose a well-allocated portfolio.

In each of the following investment categories there will be at least one investment choice available to plan participants, as selected by the plan trustees. Plan participants should be able to choose from this list in any combination they deem appropriate:

- Diversified conservative portfolio allocation
- Diversified moderate portfolio allocation
- Diversified growth portfolio allocation
- Cash or money market fund
- Large U.S. stock fund
- Small U.S. stock fund
- Non-U.S. stock fund
- Emerging market stock fund
- Real estate stock fund
- Short-term government bond fund
- Intermediate-term diversified bond fund
- High yield bond fund

FEES

All mutual funds to be used in the portfolios will be purchased at net asset value (NAV) in the share class with the lowest ongoing annual fund expenses. B- or C-type shares will not be used in these portfolios.

Selection and Retention Criteria for Investments

Mutual funds available in the 401(k) plan shall be selected on the following basis:

- PERFORMANCE RELATIVE TO PEER GROUP: Top 50% in at minimum 3 of 5 annual year rolling returns (1-, 3- and 5-year periods)

- PERFORMANCE RELATIVE TO ASSUMED RISK: Alpha and Sharpe ratios must be above the median for the asset class

- INCEPTION DATE: The fund must have a five-year track record

- CORRELATION TO PEER GROUP: There must be a positive correlation to its style-specific peer group

- ASSETS UNDER MANAGEMENT: $75 million minimum

- HOLDINGS CONSISTENT WITH STYLE: There must be at least an 80% correlation to the broad asset class

- EXPENSE RATIOS OR FEES: Must be in the 75% percentile (or in the lowest 25% of peer group funds)

- STABILITY OF THE ORGANIZATION: Each fund shall have been managed by the same person(s) or substantially the same group for at least the last twelve months.

TERMINATION OF A MANAGER

Should the investment manager determine that a manager should be terminated, one of several approaches can be used. Selection of the appropriate approach will be determined based on the least disruption for the participants.

1. Freeze the assets managed by the to-be-terminated manager and direct new assets to a replacement manager.

2. Gradually phase out the manager over a one-year period.

3. Continue offering the manager but add another peer-manager choice

4. Remove the manager and provide a replacement manager.

Investment Reports for Trustees

The trustees shall receive from the Investment Advisor no less frequently than on a quarterly basis, and within 30 days within the end of each such quarter, the following reports:

1. Performance results over the last quarter, year, 3 years and 5 years for each fund

2. Performance results of comparative benchmarks for the same periods

3. Total value of plan assets

The Advisor

Ace Checkwriter, Financial Advisors (Advisor) is a registered investment adviser and shall act as the investment advisor and fiduciary to the Investor until the Investor decides otherwise.

Advisor shall be responsible for:

1. Assisting the trustees with investment selection and monitoring in a manner consistent with this Investment Policy Statement and in accordance with state and federal law and the Uniform Prudent Investor Act.

2. Recommending an appropriate custodian to safeguard Investor's

assets.

3. Advising the Investor about the selection of and the allocation of asset categories.

4. Identifying specific assets and investment managers within each asset category.

5. Ensuring that the custodian provides Investor with a current prospectus, where applicable, for each investment proposed for the portfolio.

6. Monitoring the performance of all selected assets.

7. Recommending changes to any of the above.

8. Provide information as identified above to the plan participants according to the above schedule. Once each year, Advisor will meet with each plan participant separately, to the extent that the plan participants choose to exercise this right, for 15–30 minutes.

9. Provide semi-annual updates to the plan participants in a group meeting as determined by the plan trustees and Acme Company.

10. Preparing and presenting appropriate reports.

Advisor will not take title to any assets nor shall Advisor exercise discretionary control over any of the Investor's assets. Advisor shall be responsible only to make recommendations to the Investor and to implement investment decisions as directed by the Investor.

The Investor

Acme 401(k) Plan and its trustees (Investor) shall be responsible for:

1. The oversight of the Portfolio.

2. Defining the investment objectives and policies of the Portfolio.

3. Directing Advisor to make changes in investment policy and to oversee and to approve or disapprove Advisor's recommendations with regard to policy, guidelines, objectives and specific investments

on a timely basis.

4. Providing Advisor with all relevant information on Investor's financial conditions and risk tolerances and notifying Advisor promptly of any changes to this information.

5. Reading and understanding the information contained in the prospectus and each investment in the Portfolio.

Adoption

Adopted by the below signed:

Date:_____

Trustee(s):_____

_____

_____

Advisor:_____

IPS Statement for a Variable Life Insurance Policy Held in a Trust

Investment Policy Statement

The Thadeus Willingham Insurance Trust

December 14, 2003

Transitions Capital Management

400 State Street, Suite 2400
Little Rock, AR 11111
777-999-8888

Table of Contents

Investment Policy Discussion

What Is an Investment Policy Statement?

An investment policy outlines and prescribes a prudent and acceptable investment philosophy and defines the investment management procedures and long-term goals for the Investor.

The Need for a Written Policy

The principal reason for developing a long-term investment policy and for putting it in writing is to enable you and us to protect your portfolio from ad hoc revisions of sound long-term policy. Without an investment policy, in times of market turmoil, investors may be inclined to make ad hoc investment decisions that are inconsistent with prudent investment management principles. Your investment policy provides a well-thought-out framework from which sound investment decisions can be made.

The development of an investment policy follows the basic approach underlying financial planning: assessing your financial condition, setting goals, developing a strategy to meet the goals, implementing the strategy, regularly reviewing the results and adjusting the strategy or the implementation as circumstances dictate. In following an investment policy, you'll employ a more disciplined and systematic approach and thereby increase the probability of satisfying your investment goals.

The Uniform Prudent Investor Act ("UPIA") was approved for use in all states at the 1994 annual Conference of Commissioners on Uniform State Law and by the American Bar Association in 1995. The act is applicable to all irrevocable trusts, including irrevocable life insurance trusts (ILITs). Noncompliance with these rules can expose a trustee to significant personal liability. Being clear about the intents, purposes and processes of the trust goes a long way toward protecting the trustee and helping the beneficiaries have clear and appropriate expectations.

Key provisions of the UPIA include:

- No investment is inherently prudent or imprudent, except in how its inclusion or exclusion impacts the portfolio as a whole.

- Trustees are expected to use all reasonably available strategies to improve the risk/reward relationship of the portfolio.

- Under most circumstances, the assets of the trust must be diversified.

- Trustees are obliged to spread portfolio investments across asset classes to enhance performance and reduce risk.

- The possible effect of inflation must be considered as part of the investment strategy. As a result, use of equities is encouraged to allow the possibility that the portfolio's growth will outpace inflation.

- Fiduciaries have a duty to either demonstrate investment skill in managing trust assets or to delegate investment management to another, more qualified party.

Specific Considerations for Life Insurance Trusts

Trust-owned life insurance management should include:

- Policy monitoring—to include review of the contract, appropriateness of the death benefit, choice of Option A or B, the solvency and other issues of the life insurance company, identification of current values, status and projected values of the life insurance policy, and comparative analysis of current portfolio to alternatives available from both the current life insurance company and others meeting the trust's criteria.

- Suitability testing and restructuring criteria so that the life insurance is managed consistent with the standard care intended for any trust investment.

- An annual review of trust assets, as required under OCC Reg 9.

- Periodic meetings with the client to review the information, confirm the client's estate planning objectives and to determine any needed actions, including restoring, restructuring or replacing the policy.

- At least every five years an inforce ledger from the insurance company using the target premium for the remainder of the policy life should be requested and reviewed with the client.

- Costs should be appropriate, including:

  — Front sales load

  — Initial administrative fees

  — Ongoing monthly fees

  — Mortality and expense charges of sub-accounts

  — Fund expenses of sub-accounts

  — Total expense ratio of the sub-accounts

  — Surrender charges of the sub-accounts

  — Policy loans

  — Transfer among sub-accounts within the contract

Steps to Take to Establish an Investment Policy

1. Assess your financial situation—identify your goals and your needs

2. Determine your tolerance for risk and your time horizon

3. Develop clear objectives for the trust

4. State how the investments are expected to help meet trust objectives

5. Identify any restrictions on the portfolio and its assets

6. Determine the asset classes and mix appropriate (the "Asset Allocation") to maximize the likelihood of achieving the investment objectives at the lowest level of risk

7. Determine the investment methodology to be used with regard to investment (manager) selection, rebalancing, buy-sell disciplines, portfolio reviews and reporting, etc.

8. Implement the decisions

9. Document all investment decisions

The net effort of the written policy is to increase the likelihood that the portfolio will be able to meet the financial needs of the Investor.

Introduction

The purpose of this Investment Policy Statement (IPS) is to establish a clear understanding between Thadeus Willingham, trustee for the Thadeus Willingham Insurance Trust ("Investor") and Transitions Capital Management ("Advisor") as to the investment goals and objectives and management policies applicable to the Investor's investment portfolio ("Portfolio"). This Investment Policy Statement:

- Establishes the Investor's expectations, objectives and guidelines in the investment of the Portfolio's assets

- Creates the framework for a well-diversified asset mix that can be expected to generate acceptable long-term returns at a level of risk suitable to the Investor, including:

  — describing an appropriate risk posture for the investment of the Investor's Portfolio

  — specifying the target asset allocation policy

  — establishing investment guidelines regarding the selection of investment managers, permissible securities and diversification of assets

  — specifying the criteria for evaluating the performance of the Portfolio's assets

- Defines the responsibilities of the Investor and the Advisor

- Encourages effective communication between the investment manager(s) and the Investor

This IPS is not a contract. This investment policy has not been reviewed by any legal counsel, and the Advisor and Investor use it at their own discretion. This IPS is intended to be a summary of an investment philosophy and the procedures that provide guidance for the Investor and the Advisor. The investment policies described in this IPS should be dynamic. These policies should reflect the Investor's current status and philosophy regarding the investment of the Portfolio. These policies will be reviewed and revised periodically to ensure they adequately reflect any changes related to the Portfolio, to the Investor or the capital markets.

It is understood that there can be no guarantee about the attainment of the goals or investment objectives outlined herein.

Overview Commentary

Assets to be Considered Under this IPS

All trust assets held at Custodian referenced in this document.

Trustee . . . . .Thadeus Willingham

Trust Data . . . . The Thadeus Willingham Insurance Trust
dated 2/29/2000

Trust Federal Tax Identification Number 94-3328465

Investor Information

Client . . . . Thadeus Willingham, Trustee
The Thadeus Willingham Insurance Trust
550 Oklahoma Circle
Little Rock, AR 11111

Account Information

Acct. Title   **Approx. Value**

The Thadeus Willingham Insurance Trust $225,000
New York Life
Contract # 454-987600
Universal Variable Life Policy

Authorized Decision Maker .... Thadeus Willingham, Trustee

Investment Advisor .... Transitions Capital Management
400 State Street, #2100
Little Rock, AR 11111
415-999-8888

Insurance Agent .... Larry Life
New York Life, Little Rock office

Trust Beneficiaries .... Marilyn Willingham Thomas, daughter
Norman Willingham, son
Myrtle Willingham, daughter
Willie Willingham, son

Investor Circumstances

The Thadeus Willingham Insurance Trust ("Trust") was established February 29, 2000, by Mr. Thadeus Willingham to purchase life insurance in a death benefit amount sufficient to pay for any and all estate taxes that would be due relating to his estate upon his death as well as to provide certain other benefits to his four children. The four children are listed immediately above in order of their respective birthdates. Currently a $6 million life policy has been purchased by the Trust, effective January 25, 2003. Premiums of $300,000 per year are being paid by the Trust from annual gifts made to the Trust by Mr. Willingham.

Thadeus Willingham is 78 years old. Gladys Willingham, his wife, died in 1998 intestate. He has a net worth of approximately $18 million, of which a substantial portion is the Willingham chicken ranch. Annual income from the ranch to Mr. Willingham comes to approximately $1.5 million. The remainder of his net worth is in his two residences ($850,000), his retirement accounts and IRAs ($1.15 million) and $3 million in his investment portfolio held at Merrill Lynch's Little Rock office. The retirement accounts and the investment portfolio are being managed separately from the Insurance Trust portfolio addressed in this IPS.

In light of his ongoing income and his other liquid assets, Mr. Willingham would like to approach this life insurance aggressively, meaning that the policy will be invested to pursue the greatest possible returns, consistent with prudent investment practices.

Investment Philosophy

The basic tenets under which this portfolio will be managed include the following:

1. Modern portfolio theory, as recognized by the 1990 Nobel Prize, will be the philosophical foundation for how the portfolio will be structured and how subsequent decisions will be made. The underlying concepts of modern portfolio theory include:

   - Investors are risk averse. The only acceptable risk is that which is adequately compensated by potential portfolio returns.

   - Markets are efficient. It is virtually impossible to anticipate the future direction of the market as a whole or of any individual security. It is, therefore, unlikely that any portfolio will succeed in consistently "beating the market."

   - The design of the portfolio as a whole is more important than the selection of any particular security within the portfolio. The appropriate allocation of capital among asset classes (stocks, bonds, cash, etc.) will have far more influence on long-term portfolio results than the selection of individual securities. Investing for the long term (preferably longer than ten years) becomes critical to investment success because it allows the long-term characteristics of the asset classes to surface.

- For a given risk level, an optimal combination of asset classes will maximize returns. Diversification helps reduce investment volatility. The proportional mix of asset classes determines the long-term risk and return characteristics of the portfolio as a whole.

- Portfolio risk can be decreased by increasing diversification of the portfolio and by lowering the correlation of market behavior among the asset classes selected. (Correlation is the statistical term for the extent to which two asset classes move in tandem or opposition to one another.)

2. Investing globally helps to minimize overall portfolio risk due to the imperfect correlation between economies of the world. Investing globally has also been shown historically to enhance portfolio returns, although there is no guarantee that it will do so in the future.

3. Equities offer the potential for higher long-term investment returns than cash or fixed income investments. Equities are also more volatile in their performance. Investors seeking higher rates of return must increase the proportion of equities in their portfolio, while at the same time accepting greater variation of results (including occasional declines in value).

Given these tenets, the underlying approach to managing this portfolio shall be to optimize the risk/return relationship appropriate to Investor's needs and goals. The portfolio will be diversified globally employing a variety of asset classes. Mutual funds or managed portfolios will be employed to implement the portfolio and the chosen asset classes will be periodically rebalanced to maintain a more consistent risk/reward profile.

Investment Objectives

To maximize the growth of the insurance policy cash values, within prudent investment practices.

Time Horizon

For the purposes of planning, the time horizon for the investments in this portfolio will parallel the lifetime of Thadeus Willingham. It is assumed that the investment horizon for this portfolio greatly exceeds ten (10) years.

Capital values do fluctuate over shorter periods and the Investor should recognize that the possibility of capital loss does exist. However, historical asset class return data suggest that the risk of principal loss over a holding period of at least three to five years can be minimized with the long-term investment mix employed under this Investment Policy Statement.

Tax Policy

Taxation is, for the most part, not a consideration in this Portfolio, although normal four-tier accounting will apply to the Trust assets.

Risk Tolerance

There are two primary factors that affect the Investor's risk tolerance:

- Financial capacity to accept risk within the investment program
- Willingness to accept return volatility.

Personal Financial Capacity

Given other assets and income, Investor has considerable financial capacity to take on risk.

Willingness to Tolerate Volatility

The Investor desires long-term investment growth. The Investor understands that to achieve such growth, the Portfolio will experience periods of decline. He further understands that in a severe market, the potential recovery period could exceed three years.

Investor prefers to accept the volatility inherent in an aggressively invested portfolio in order to improve the growth possibilities.

Taking these two factors into account, the Investor's risk tolerance may be characterized as aggressive.

Asset Allocation

Academic research offers considerable evidence that the asset allocation decision far outweighs security selection and market timing in its impact on portfolio performance. After reviewing the long-term performance and risk characteristics of various asset classes and balancing the risk and rewards of market behavior, the following asset classes were selected to achieve the objectives of the Investor's Portfolio.

ASSET ALLOCATION			
CATEGORY	HOLDINGS	RANGE	NORMAL
Cash		**1–5%**	**1%**
	Taxable Money Market Funds	1–5%	1%
Bonds		**0–30%**	**9%**
	Corporate Bonds	0–30%	9%
Stocks		**50–88%**	**84%**
	U.S. Large Stocks	20–40%	35%
	U.S. Small Stocks	7–25%	20%
	International Stocks	15–30%	20%
	Emerging Market Stocks	2–15%	9%
Real Estate		**2–10%**	**6%**
	REITs	2–10%	6%
TOTAL		**100%**	**100%**

Historical Portfolio Returns & Volatility

The following historical returns reflect the results of this Portfolio, as normally constructed, over the 1972 to 200X time period.

Bear in mind, these outcomes represent historical results using index data and estimated expenses. It should be recognized that the Portfolio will invest in mutual funds or other securities and that the actual weighting of these securities can and will vary. It is also important to note that the future returns of the securities with the Portfolio can be expected to vary from the historical returns referenced.

The Portfolio results referenced reflect a portfolio design having a "value" orientation (i.e., employing funds or stocks with below-average price to book ratios). Historically, over-weighting "value" investments in a portfolio has resulted in higher portfolio returns with lower risk when compared to portfolios with greater "growth" characteristics. The Investor's Portfolio will be designed with a "value" orientation.

The Portfolio's historical rate of return is not a guarantee of future investment returns. Future returns could differ significantly and capital loss is possible. This Investment Policy Statement shall not be construed as offering a guarantee.

Historical Portfolio & Asset Class Returns (1972 to 200X)

ASSET CLASS	HISTORICAL RETURN	STANDARD DEVIATION
Portfolio Return (geometric mean)	12.8%	14.4%
Less Estimated Expenses	1.7%	
Portfolio Return (net)	11.1%	
Less Inflation (5.0% + 0.3% compounding)	5.3%	1.2%
Real Return After Inflation	5.8%	
Asset Class Returns (before expenses):		
Cash	6.6%	0.8%
Intermediate Bonds	8.5%	4.9%
U.S. Large Stocks	12.2%	17.5%
U.S. Small Stocks	13.3%	24.8%
International Stocks	11.2%	19.1%
Emerging Market Stocks*	11.3%	27.8%
Real Estate	12.5%	15.4%

* Emerging Market data since 1988

Historical Rolling Period Real Returns (1972 to 2003)

	ROLLING ONE-YEAR PERIODS	ROLLING FIVE-YEAR PERIODS
Annualized Returns:		
Best Periods	42.0%	21.0%
Average (arithmetic mean)	5.4%	6.3%
Worst Period	−35.2%	−4.4%
% of Periods generating:		
Negative Returns	27.2%	9.3%
Less than CPI + 4%	47.3%	30.9%

The returns reflected above are *after* inflation and include price appreciation, dividends, interest and are net of 1.7% estimated mutual fund management expenses and advisory fees. They assume use of taxable bonds (municipal bonds yield less but are assumed to return about the same after taxes). Calculations do not include the impact of transaction costs or income taxes.

Updated Allocations

The allocation, as identified above, allows for a range of allocations within each asset class. Advisor shall retain and Investor grants Advisor the right to make changes within the range(s) specified as Advisor determines appropriate based on Advisor's sole insight with regards to the economy, the markets and the general investing environment. Changes shall be made by Advisor with the intent of enhancing the likelihood of the portfolio attaining the objectives as stated above.

At all times a target asset allocation shall exist and Investor shall be so notified by Advisor of changes to target.

Over time, it may be desirable to amend the basic allocation policy or calculations. When such changes are made, updates will be attached to this Investment Policy Statement as an Appendix and will be considered part of this Investment Policy Statement.

Rebalancing Procedures

From time to time, market conditions may cause the Portfolio's investment in various asset classes to vary from the established allocation. To remain consistent with the asset allocation guidelines established by this Investment Policy Statement and as established in writing by Advisor, every quarter the Advisor shall review the Portfolio and each asset class in which the Portfolio is invested. If the actual weighting differs from the target weighting by 5% or more from the recommended weighting (e.g., from a recommended 10% to less than 5% or more than 15% of total assets) the Advisor shall rebalance the Portfolio back to the recommended weighting. Such rebalancing shall be limited to securities previously approved by Investor.

Frequency of Review

The Investor recognizes that all investments go through cycles and, therefore, there will be periods of time in which the investment objectives are not met or when specific managers fail to meet their expected performance expectations.

The Investor accepts the principle that, in the absence of specific circumstances requiring immediate action, patience and a longer-term perspective will be employed when evaluating investment performance.

On an overall Portfolio basis, the Investor establishes a goal of evaluating Portfolio investment performance relative to investment benchmarks over a minimum time period of five years.

Advisor and Investor should review this Investment Policy Statement together every two years.

Liquidity

No cash distributions are anticipated from this trust so all capital gains paid and interest can be reinvested.

Diversification

Investment choices for this Portfolio will of necessity be limited by the availability of choices within the insurance policy held within the trust, including all sub-accounts. All choices included as sub-account alternatives within the policy shall be available for utilization within this portfolio. Investment alternatives not available as sub-accounts to this insurance policy may not be included.

Investment Management Selection

Investment managers (including mutual funds, money managers and limited partnership sponsors) shall be chosen using the following criteria:

- Past performance, considered relative to other investments having the same investment objective. Consideration shall be given to both performance rankings over various time frames and consistency of performance.

- Costs relative to other funds with like objectives and investment styles.

- The manager's adherence to investment style and size objectives.

- Size of the proposed mutual fund.

- Length of time the fund has been in existence and length of time it has been under the direction of the current manager(s) and whether or not there have been material changes in the manager's organization and personnel.

- The historical volatility and downside risk of each proposed investment.

- How well each proposed investment complements other assets in the Portfolio.

- The current economic environment.

- Investment monitoring and control procedures

Reports

1. The insurance company shall provide Investor with quarterly statements for the account, listing all assets held by Investor, values for each asset and all transactions affecting assets within the Portfolio, including additions and withdrawals.

2. Transitions Capital Management shall provide Investor no less frequently than on an annual basis, and within 30 days within the end of each such calendar year, the following management reports:

   a) Portfolio performance results over the last year

   b) Performance results of each individual holding for the year

   c) End of year status regarding asset allocation—current versus policy

   d) Any recommendations for changes of the above

Meetings and Communication Between Investor and Advisor

As a matter of course, Transitions Capital Management shall keep Investor apprised of any material changes in Transitions Capital Management's outlook, recommended investment policy, and tactics. In addition, Transitions Capital Management shall meet with Investor approximately annually to review and explain the Portfolio's investment results and any related issues. Transitions Capital Management shall also be available on a reasonable basis for telephone and e-mail communication as needed.

Any material event that affects the ownership of Transitions Capital Management's firm or the management of the Portfolio must be reported immediately to Investor.

Duties and Responsibilities

The Advisor

Transitions Capital Management is expected to manage the Portfolio in a manner consistent with this Investment Policy Statement and in accordance with state and federal law and the Uniform Prudent Investor Act. Transitions Capital Management is a registered investment adviser and shall act as the investment advisor and fiduciary to the Investor until the Investor decides otherwise.

Transitions Capital Management shall be responsible for:

1. Designing, recommending and implementing an appropriate asset allocation plan consistent with the investment objectives, time horizon, risk profile, guidelines and constraints outlined in this statement

2. Advising the Investor about the selection of and the allocation of investments

3. Monitoring the performance of all selected assets

4. Recommending changes to any of the above

5. Periodically reviewing the suitability of the investments for the Investor

6. Being available to meet with the Investor at least annually, and being available at such other times within reason at the Investor's request

7. Preparing and presenting appropriate reports

Discretion and Title

Investor grants Transitions Capital Management discretionary control for purchases and sales of securities previously approved by Investor. Advisor shall have no authority to withdraw funds from Investor's accounts, except to cover payment of previously agreed-to fees or at Investor's specific direction.

The Investor

Investor shall be responsible for:

1. The oversight of the Portfolio

2. Defining the investment objectives and policies of the Portfolio

3. Directing Transitions Capital Management to make changes in investment policy and to oversee and to approve or disapprove Transitions Capital Management's recommendations with regard to policy, guidelines, objectives and specific investments on a timely basis.

4. Providing Transitions Capital Management with all relevant information on Investor's financial conditions and risk tolerances and notifying Transitions Capital Management promptly of any changes to this information

5. Investor shall read and understand the information contained in the prospectus and each investment in the Portfolio

6. Investor is responsible for exercising all rights, including voting rights, as are acquired through the purchase of securities

Adoption

Adopted by the below signed:

Date:_____

Investor:_____

_____

Advisor:_____

IPS Executive Summary for File

Thadeus Willingham Insurance Trust

Original IPS Date: January 20, 2003

Amended on: _____

Investor .... The Thadeus Willingham Insurance Trust
dtd 2/29/2000
Thadeus Willingham, Trustee

Tax ID Number 94-3328465

Insurance Policy .... New York Life
Contract # 454-987600
Universal Variable Life Policy

Investment Objective: aggressive growth

Time Horizon: Well over ten years

Risk Tolerance: Moderate

ASSET ALLOCATION	NORMAL	RANGE
Money Market Funds	1%	1–5%
Corporate Bonds	9%	5–30%
U.S. Large Stocks	35%	20–40%
U.S. Small Stocks	20%	7–15%
International Stocks	20%	15–39%
Emerging Market Stocks	9%	2–15%
REITs	6%	2–10%
TOTAL	100%	100%

Note: Within the above allocation, the following broad limits will apply:

- Bonds and cash to never exceed 35% nor to fall below 10% in aggregate

- Stocks, including REITs, to never exceed 90% nor to fall below 65%

EXPECTED PORTFOLIO RETURN CHARACTERISTICS		
ASSET CLASS	HISTORICAL RETURN	STANDARD DEVIATION
Historical Portfolio Return (geometric mean)	11.8%	11.4%
Less Estimated Expenses	1.7%	
Historical Portfolio Return (net)	10.1%	
Best One-Year Period 1972-2003	42.0%	
Worst One-Year Period 1972-2003	−35.2%	

Sample Executive Summary for File

We are providing the reader a sample of an executive summary of what we believe are the relevant issues for the client. Some advisors include this summary in the complete Investment Policy Statement that is given to the client as we have with a couple of earlier sample IPSs. Some may choose to use this as a summary document to distribute to staff, put in the client file as a quick resource or for other snapshot purposes.

IPS Executive Summary for File

Robert Jones CRT

Original IPS Date: December 1, 200X

Amended on: _____

Investor   The Robert Jones CRT, Robert Jones Trustee

Tax ID Number 94-3327744

Custodian: . . . . .Charles Schwab & Co.
                                                    Account #12345678

Investment Objective: pre-tax average annual return of 4.0% above
    inflation

Time Horizon: Well over ten years

Risk Tolerance: Moderate

ASSET ALLOCATION	NORMAL	RANGE
Money Market Funds	1%	1–5%
Corporate Bonds	29%	19–45%
U.S. Large Stocks	27%	20–40%
U.S. Small Stocks	12%	7–15%
International Stocks	22%	15–25%
Emerging Market Stocks	5%	2–10%
REITs	4%	2–10%
TOTAL	100%	100%

Note: Within the above allocation, the following broad limits will apply:

- Bonds and cash to never exceed 50% nor to fall below 20% in
  aggregate

- Stocks, including REITs, to never exceed 80% nor to fall below 50%

EXPECTED PORTFOLIO RETURN CHARACTERISTICS

ASSET CLASS	HISTORICAL RETURN	STANDARD DEVIATION
Historical Portfolio Return (geometric mean)	11.8%	11.4%
Less Estimated Expenses	1.7%	
Historical Portfolio Return (net)	10.1%	1.2%
Less Inflation (5.0% + 0.3% compounding)	5.3%	
Historical Real Return After Inflation	4.8%	
Best One-Year Period 1972–2003	42.0%	
Worst One-Year Period 1972–2003	–35.2%	

Printed in the United States
135839LV00003BA/49/A

9 780975 344804